Dictionary of
CANVAS
WORK
STITCHES

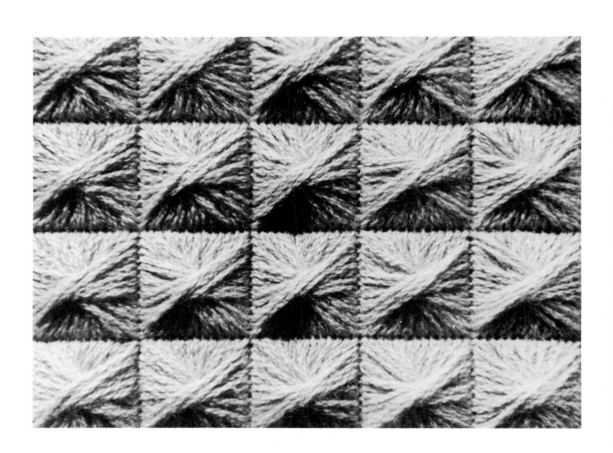

Dictionary of CANVAS WORK STITCHES

Mary Rhodes

CHARLES SCRIBNER'S SONS
NEW YORK

Acknowledgment

I should like to express my deep gratitude to all
my students who so cheerfully and willingly
helped me in working the numerous samples of
the stitches in this book, also to my many
American friends who helped to test out the diagrams of these stitches in the workshops on
Canvas Embroidery, which we did together during
my two wonderful tours of the United States.
Among the latter I should especially like to thank
Muriel Baker for drawing my attention to Dutch
Stitch. Finally, I have to thank my husband, Val,
for the immense amount of help he has given me,
not only in typing the text, in photographing all
the stitches and in assisting me in checking the
proofs of the manuscript, but also for actually
working some of the stitch-models himself, which
by the way, was his first venture into the Art of
Canvas Embroidery.

MR
Eltham, London 1980

© Mary Rhodes 1980
First U.S. edition published by
Charles Scribner's Sons, 1980

1 3 5 7 9 11 13 15 17 19 I/C 20 18 16 14 12 10 8 6 4 2

Printed in Great Britain
Library of Congress Catalog Number 80 — 50909
ISNB 0-684-16669-0

INTRODUCTION

Since I started compiling this dictionary, I have been truly amazed at the number of stitches which are available to the canvas-worker. There are stitches for all purposes, some of which are large — even very large — and some small; there are some very old stitches, and some which are completely new; there are some stitches which, it must be admitted, are less suitable than others in providing what used to be considered an adequate covering of the canvas, but even these have their place in modern canvas work, where it is now considered acceptable not to cover every thread of the canvas with stitchery.

The list of suitable stitches is constantly being added to in various ways. People are always looking at other branches of embroidery for inspiration, and they borrow ideas from one another in their desire to find something new to use in their work. Many stitches, which have been included in this book, such as Stem, Portuguese Stem and Palestrina, were always thought of in the past as crewel-work stitches, but for some time now they have been used very successfully on canvas and are consequently accepted today as part of the canvas-work scene. Often stitches come into being by mistake: someone will try to work a certain stitch, fail to work it correctly, and come up with another stitch, which, although different, is just as attractive. Cretan Stitch Variation is an example of this.

This constant development of new canvas work stitches, which is occurring over a very wide area of the world, makes it impossible for me to claim to have included in this book all the existing stitches which can be used on canvas. I ask for indulgence, therefore, from anyone whose favourite stitch has been omitted from my list. The fact that canvas work is carried out by many people living far apart from one another, and not all speaking the same language, can also lead to a great variety of names being used for what is in reality the same stitch. I have given the stitches the name by which I have known them over a very long period of time, so that Florentine Stitch, for instance, remains for me Florentine, and not Bargello or Irish Stitch, and Rice Stitch remains Rice, and not William and Mary, or any other name that may have been thought up for it. I have, nevertheless, mentioned, as far as possible, the alternative names for all the well-known stitches, but I am bound, unfortunately, to have omitted some.

My hope is that everyone who uses this book will be inspired to experiment with stitches and not be content simply to use them as they are diagrammed. It is permissible to play around with them, to enlarge them and to try to elongate some of the square stitches. If some of the stitches appear to be too thin, and empty intersections of the canvas are left between them, it is not always necessary to unpick the work and start again with a thicker yarn, or use a different stitch. The worker may instead try to overwork the existing piece with extra stitches, using the same or a different yarn. The procedure adopted must be the same for each stitch, so that a regular pattern of stitches will eventually be evolved. I can assure you that there is great fun to be had from experimenting, and who knows what gem of a stitch may thus be born!

Algerian Double Eye

In working this version of Algerian Eye Stitch a similar method to that used for Algerian Eye is employed, but each of the eight original individual stitches is worked twice to give sixteen individual stitches going into the central hole. The effect would not be the same if a double thread of yarn were used in working this stitch, instead of doing each of the original individual stitches twice.

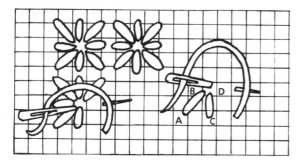

Algerian Eye

This stitch covers a square of four threads of the canvas each way and it gives the same effect if worked either in straight rows or diagonally across the canvas.

Each stitch consists of a group of eight individual stitches which are brought up from points round the edge of the square and taken down into the centre hole. The yarn used should be pulled as tightly as possible in order to accentuate this central hole, and care must be taken to work in such a way, that the hole in the finished stitch will not be obstructed by threads of yarn on the back of the work. Some people prefer to work the top half of the stitches first, when they are going to cover an area of canvas with this stitch: they start working from the right-hand side and progress horizontally across the canvas and then complete the lower half of each stitch by working back from left to right. This method ensures that the correct tension will be maintained and it avoids any danger of obstructing the central hole in the stitch by threads on the back.

Algerian Eye Overlapped Filling

This variation of Algerian Eye Stitch is achieved by working the Overlapping Border Variation with additional horizontal stitches to cover the divisions between the rows of eye stitches and thus produce an unbroken all-over filling stitch.

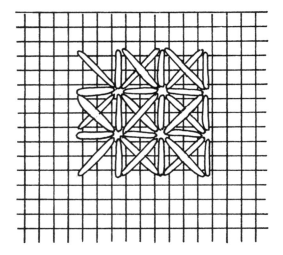

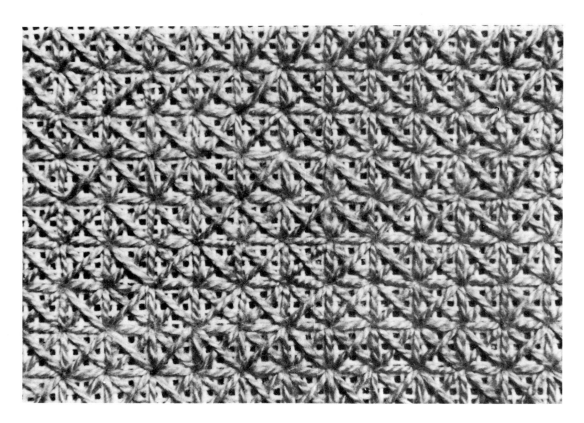

Algerian Eye Overlapping Border

This is another variation of the Algerian Eye Stitch in which extra stitches are worked in the spaces between the individual eye stitches, thus producing an overlapping effect, which increases the weight of the horizontal rows of stitches in a way which is useful in forming an attractive border pattern. It can also be used as an all-over filling stitch.

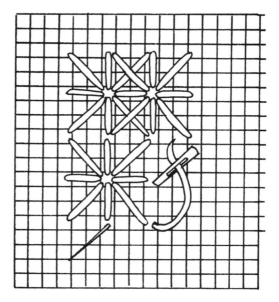

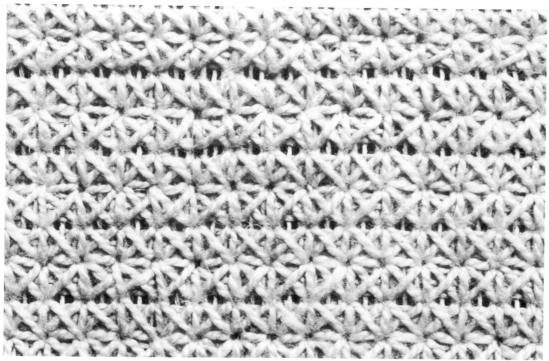

Algerian Eye Variation

Here the same eight individual stitches of a normal Algerian Eye Stitch alternate with eight smaller stitches, each one over one intersection of the canvas. For greater ease in working this stitch it is advisable to work these smaller stitches first and then put in the longer ones between them. As a result of this, it is necessary to complete each single eyelet stitch before proceeding to the next. A thicker yarn is also generally used for this variation and it is not pulled so tightly, with the result that the centre hole is less prominent here than in normal Algerian Eye Stitch.

All of the stitches in this group can be worked both as individual stitches and as blocks of filling stitches.

See also *Eyelet* Stitch

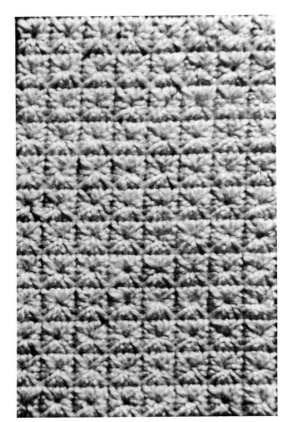

Algerian Filling

This filling stitch consists of groups of three vertical straight stitches, worked over four horizontal threads of the canvas. To work it horizontally across the canvas, one should begin by working

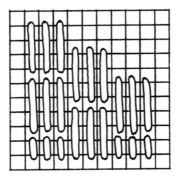

a row of these groups of three vertical stitches in such a way that a space of four vertical and four horizontal threads of the canvas is left between them. The next row of stitches is then placed in the spaces left between the first row, but with a half-drop, which means that the needle is brought up two horizontal threads of the canvas down from the top of the first stitch and one vertical thread to one side of it. To work this stitch diagonally across the canvas, each group of three vertical stitches should be placed beside the group worked before it, but two horizontal threads of the canvas above or below the line on which the previous group began.

Algerian Filling with bar

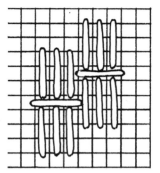

Algerian Plaited

The effect of this stitch when worked is similar to that of Herringbone Stitch and Plait Stitch, but the method of working is slightly different. The needle is brought up at the top left-hand corner of the area to be covered and is taken down diagonally over six horizontal threads and four vertical threads of the canvas to the right. It is then taken back to the left under the canvas for three vertical threads and again brought up to make a diagonal stitch upwards over six horizontal and five vertical threads to the right. Finally, the needle is taken back under the canvas for three vertical threads, and the whole process can begin once more.

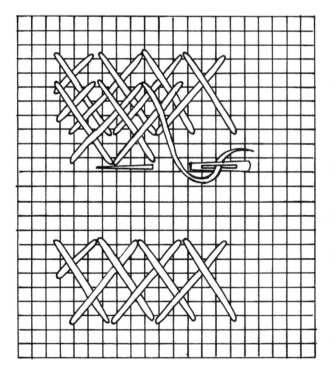

Arrow

This stitch starts with the working of three vertical straight stitches over four threads of the canvas. The needle is then brought out beside this initial

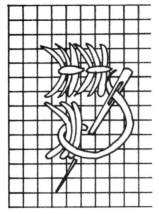

group of stitches at a point which is two threads of the canvas down and one thread to the right. Having been passed under these stitches (but not through the canvas), the needle with the yarn is brought back over them and down into the same hole in the canvas from where it emerged, thus pulling the stitches tightly to one side. The first stitch of the next group of three straight stitches shares the same hole in the canvas as the last straight stitch of the previous group.

Arrow Stitch can also be worked over six horizontal threads of the canvas, but it then has groups of five vertical straight stitches each time instead of three, and the loop encircling the stitches is brought up and taken down again two threads of the canvas to the right of the group, and not one.

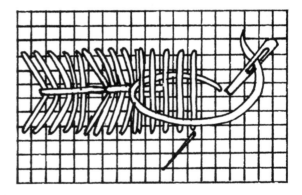

Arrow Half-drop Filling

When this stitch is used as an all-over filling stitch, there is a half-drop between adjoining groups of straight stitches, and they are pulled alternately to the left and to the right. The working can be carried out horizontally, vertically or diagonally across the canvas.

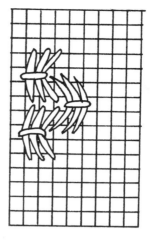

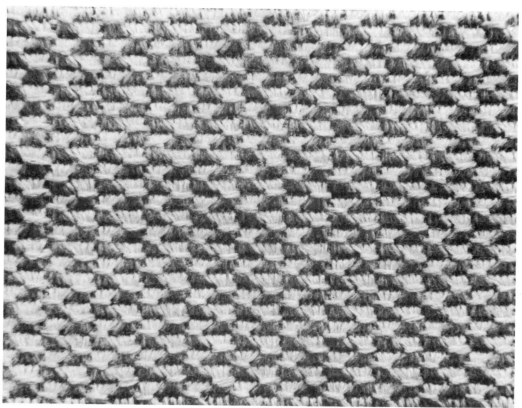

Aubusson. See Rep

Back (Also known as Point de Sable)

This stitch is very useful for working between areas of other stitches, where some bare canvas threads may need covering. It is always worked between threads of the canvas and itself generally covers two threads. The needle is taken under two empty threads of the canvas, emerges and is brought back over the same two threads, whence it passes under the worked back stitch and on under two further empty threads to form a second back stitch and continue in the same way as required. Back Stitch is sometimes worked over only one thread, which make it, together with Tent Stitch, one of the smallest stitches for canvas work.

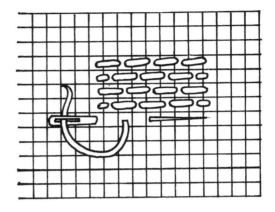

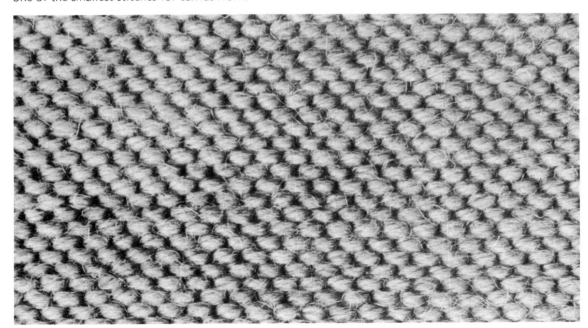

Back Filling

The photograph of Back Stitch shows it worked as a filling stitch in its own right. It is an attractive stitch to use in this way, when a light, open effect is needed.

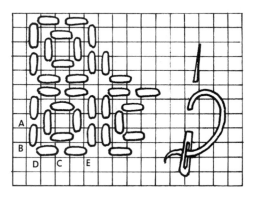

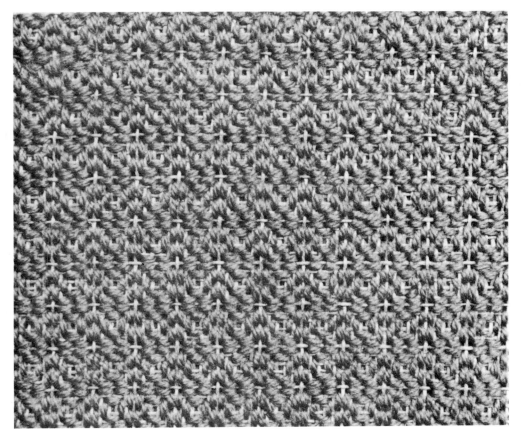

Balcony

This stitch, which is similar in construction to Broad Cross, is a very quick stitch to work, and it covers the canvas well. Five vertical straight stitches are taken down over twelve horizontal threads of the canvas, and these are crossed by five horizontal straight stitches of the same length, starting at a point four horizontal threads of the canvas down from the top of the first vertical stitch and four vertical threads to the left. The individual groups of stitches are worked diagonally across the area to be covered and are fitted together into a close pattern.

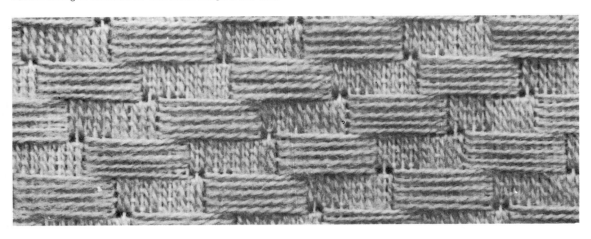

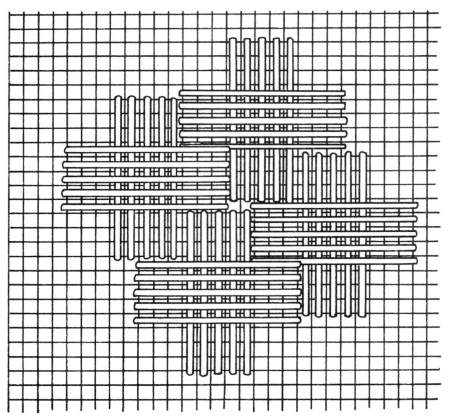

Barred Beetle. See Beetle, Barred

Basket Filling

This stitch consists of alternate groups of horizontal and vertical straight stitches, forming a basket pattern. The number of straight stitches in each group shown in the photograph is five and they are worked over six threads of the canvas, but these figures may be varied, if it is so desired: for example, three straight stitches can be worked over four threads of the canvas or four stitches over five threads, and so on.

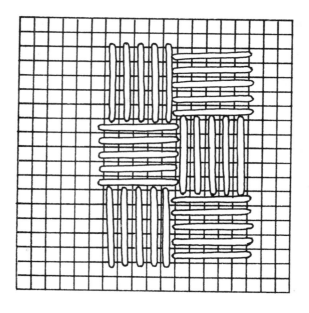

Beetle

This stitch consists of a group of eight horizontal straight stitches, worked over a central group of three vertical straight stitches. The eight horizontal stitches are varied in length, the first at the top being worked over four threads of the canvas, followed by one horizontal stitch over six threads, four over eight threads, another one over six threads and the final one at the bottom of the group over four threads of the canvas. The group of three vertical stitches, which underlie the centre of the main stitch-group, serve as padding to build up the final shape.

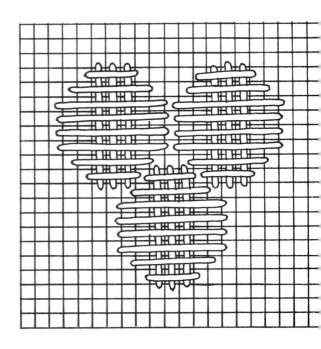

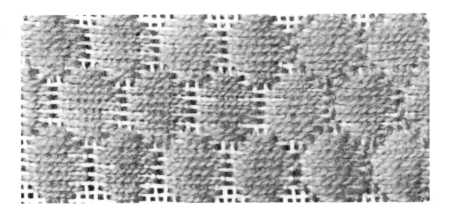

Beetle, Barred

In this variation of Beetle Stitch the group of
eight horizontal straight stitches has been increased
to ten individual stitches by the addition of two
further horizontal straight stitches, each one
over two vertical threads of the canvas, one of
which is placed immediately above and one
immediately beneath the original group of eight
horizontal straight stitches. These ten stitches are
put in first without any padding beneath them,
and then three vertical stitches are taken over
them. All three of these vertical stitches emerge
from the centre hole at the base of the original
group of stitches, one horizontal thread of the
canvas below the last stitch; one of these vertical
stitches is taken up over eleven horizontal threads
of the canvas and into the centre hole above the
first stitch; the other two stitches go up over ten
horizontal threads of the canvas and into the holes
at either end of the first stitch.

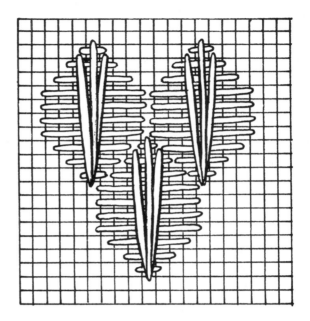

Bokhara Couching

One strand of wool is used to work this stitch, both for the laid thread and for the stitches holding it down. The needle should be brought out at the top left-hand corner of the area to be worked and the yarn taken across to the right between two horizontal threads of the canvas. The needle is then taken down through the canvas and brought up two vertical threads back to the left, where it is taken over the laid thread and down over one intersection of the canvas to the right. This stitch ties down the laid thread, and it is repeated four vertical threads of the canvas further to the left, the process being repeated at the same intervals along the full length of the laid thread. Other horizontal threads of yarn are tied down in this way as required, but the position of the first tie-stitch from the end of each laid thread alternates between two and four vertical threads of the canvas.

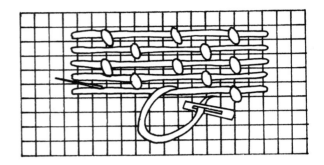

Blanket. See Buttonhole

Bouclé

This is a square stitch, which can be worked over any number of threads of the canvas, provided that the yarn used is matched to the size of the stitch. A row of diagonal stitches, each one worked from the bottom left-hand corner to the top right-hand corner of its square, is first put in across the top of the area to be covered, with these stitches being firmly tensioned. The yarn is then brought up through the canvas at the top left-hand corner of each stitch, and a loop is taken over the diagonal stitch, before the needle is returned back down through the same hole in the canvas from which it had emerged. A second row of diagonal stitches is then put in beside the original ones, each new diagonal stitch coming up through the same hole and going down into the

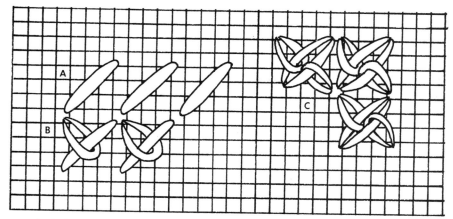

same hole in the canvas as one of the first diagonal stitches. These diagonal stitches also need to be firmly tensioned, as the others were. The yarn is then brought up through the canvas at the bottom right-hand corner of each square stitch and is taken in a loop over the new diagonal stitch and

down again into the same hole in the canvas from which it had emerged. In order to obtain the correct bouclé effect, it is essential that all the loops used in working this stitch should be left slack and not tensioned in the way the diagonal stitches were.

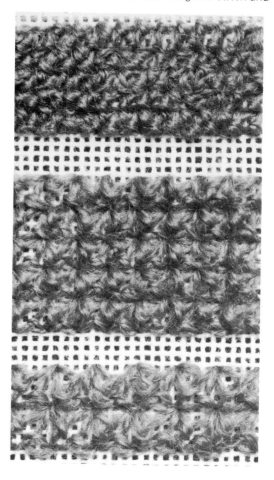

Braid (Also known as Gordian Knot Stitch)

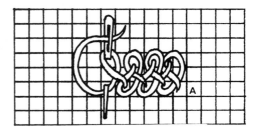

This stitch is worked horizontally from right to left. The diagram shows it being worked over two horizontal threads of the canvas, but it can be worked over any number of threads, as the photograph shows. One should begin by bringing the needle up through the canvas at a point on the lower edge of the stitch. A loop of the working yarn is then placed in the position shown in the diagram and held there on the canvas with the left thumb, whilst the needle is inserted through the loop and taken down through the canvas at a point which is two horizontal threads up from where the stitch began and one vertical thread to the left. The needle is brought out again two horizontal threads of the canvas down, where it is then ready to begin the next stitch. The loop of yarn should be pulled tight around the needle, before the latter is finally drawn out.

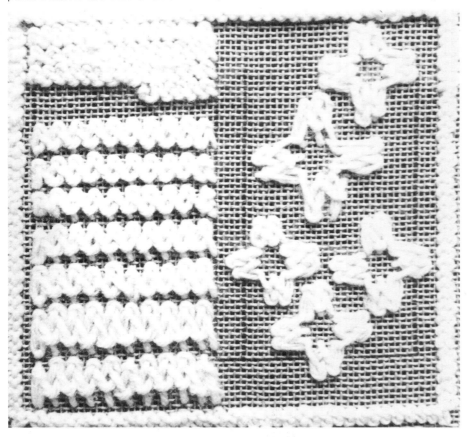

Brazilian (Ponto Rosinhas)

This stitch is worked over four horizontal and four vertical threads of the canvas and is based on Long-legged Cross Stitch. The first part of the stitch is worked solely over the first two threads of the canvas, as in Long-legged Cross. The fifth and subsequent movements of the needle are made over the next two threads of the canvas, starting at the top, and an inverted Long-legged Cross is worked. The diagram shows clearly the position of the needle at different stages in the working of the stitch, and it should be watched carefully, whilst one is learning how to proceed. Once the order of the stitches has been memorised, Brazilian Stitch is reasonably quick to work.

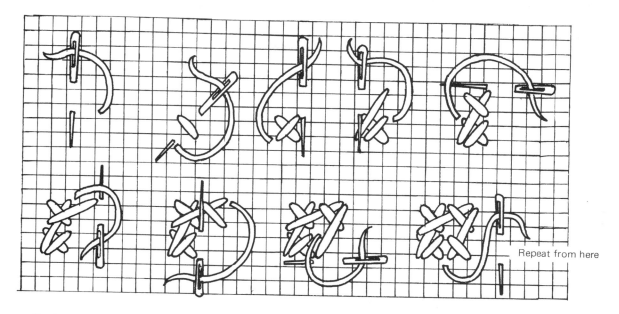

Repeat from here

Small — worked over four horizontal threads

Large — worked over eight horizontal threads

Brick

This stitch consists of blocks of three horizontal stitches over six vertical threads of the canvas, placed side by side from left to right across the canvas, and having immediately beneath them blocks of two rows of horizontal stitches over two vertical threads of the canvas, with the first block of two rows of horizontal stitches starting one vertical thread of the canvas to the right of the point where the first block of three horizontal stitches begins.

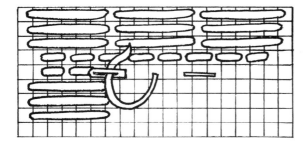

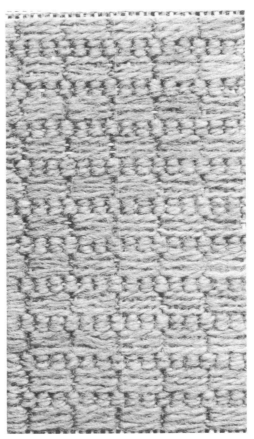

Brick Filling

This stitch consists of blocks of two horizontal stitches worked over four vertical threads of the canvas, with a vertical back stitch over two horizontal threads worked between the blocks. The horizontal stitches should be worked first, and the vertical back stitch added afterwards. A variation of this stitch can be obtained by working single stitches horizontally over six vertical threads of the canvas, alternating with one horizontal stitch over two vertical threads. On the return row the small stitch comes in the centre of the large stitch of the preceding row.

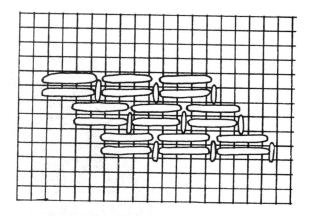

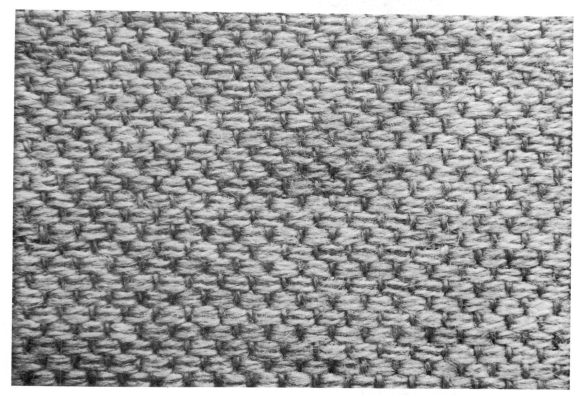

Bricking, Fancy

This is similar to Brick Stitch, but the blocks of stitches in the first row are smaller, being worked over three vertical threads of the canvas instead of six, and beneath them are groups of two vertical stitches over three horizontal threads of the canvas, interspersed with blocks of two horizontal stitches over two vertical threads of the canvas.

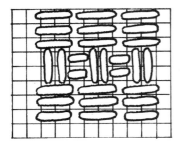

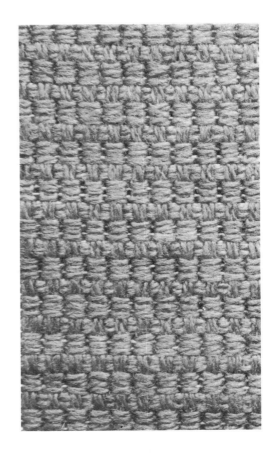

Broad Cross

This very attractive stitch occupies a square of six threads of the canvas. Three vertical stitches over six threads of the canvas are worked first, and then the three horizontal stitches are put in across them by bringing the needle up for the first stitch at a point two horizontal threads of the canvas down and two vertical threads to the left of where the first vertical stitch began. To work the second row of Broad Crosses the easiest method is to start by working the centre stitch of the three vertical stitches: this is done by bringing the needle up six horizontal threads of the canvas down from where the third horizontal stitch in the first Broad Cross began and six vertical threads to the right. The needle then goes down into the same hole in the canvas as the third horizontal stitch in the first and second Broad Crosses in the first row. A stitch is then put in on either side of this middle vertical stitch and the whole Broad Cross is completed as in the diagram.

A variation of this stitch can be worked, if desired, by putting in the three horizontal stitches first and then working the vertical ones across them.

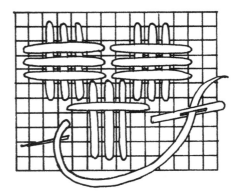

Broad Cross — Diagonal

When this stitch is worked on the diagonal, each complete cross occupies a square of seven threads of the canvas. It takes the same form as when it is worked horizontally, but individual stitches follow the line of the true diagonal of the canvas and are taken over five intersections. As in the horizontal version of the stitch, it is possible to work either group of three parallel stitches first, with the other group of three stitches worked over them.

In both forms of Broad Cross the size of the stitch may be varied.

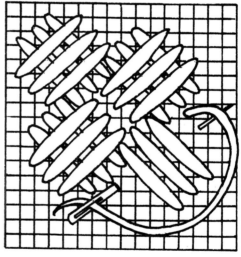

Bullion (Also known as Caterpillar, Coil, Knot, Porto Rico Rose, Post, Roll and Worm)

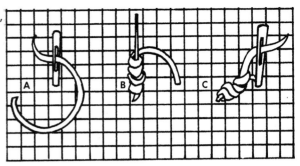

The working thread is brought up through the canvas at point A, where the Bullion Stitch is to begin, and is taken down again at a point which will give the length of stitch required — point B in the diagram — but leaving the thread as loose as possible on the surface of the canvas between these points. The tip of the needle is then brought up again through the canvas at point A and held in a vertical position with the left hand, whilst the working thread is taken in the right hand and wrapped several times around the tip of the needle, the number of times depending upon the length of the stitch being worked. The left hand is then brought up to the surface to hold the coil of thread close to the canvas, whilst with the right hand the needle is eased gently through the canvas and the coil of thread. This coil continues to be held in position whilst the loose working thread is pulled through it and taken down through the canvas again at point B.

Bullion stitches are often used for overworking on top of Tent Stitch or other small stitches. They are also ideal for working texture in designs such as those depicting landscapes.

The 'Porto Rico Rose' is formed by working a number of Bullion Stitches in a coil to resemble a flower.

The photograph also shows the slightly different way of working this stitch, when the canvas is not on a frame, but is being held in the hand.

Buttonhole

There are many variations of Buttonhole Stitch, of which only a few have been shown in the diagrams. The first one shown is the simplest form of the stitch, which is worked from left to right across the canvas. A series of vertical straight stitches over three or more horizontal threads of the canvas is put in, starting with the working yarn being brought out at the bottom left-hand corner of the area to be covered. The needle is then in-serted at the point which is to be the top of the first stitch and is taken down under the canvas to emerge one thread to the right of where the working yarn was first brought out. It is then taken over the loop of this yarn, thus holding it down close to the canvas, and the second stitch is worked. When a complete row of Buttonhole Stitches has been worked, it is necessary to put in one more straight stitch at the beginning of the row in order to fill up the space.

A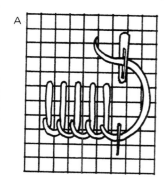

B

C

Buttonhole or Blanket

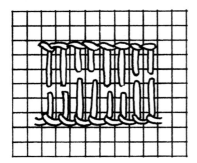

Buttonhole Border

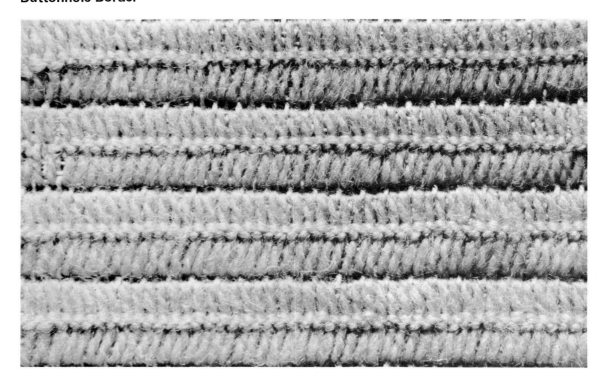

Buttonhole Filling, Open

This stitch begins at the top left-hand corner of the area to be covered, and a row of overlapping loop stitches is worked from left to right. The working yarn is taken over four vertical threads of the canvas and is left loose, whilst the needle is taken back under two vertical threads and is brought up to pass over the first stitch and continue in the same way with the next stitches. The second row of stitches is worked into the loops of the first row, and subsequent rows continue in the same way.

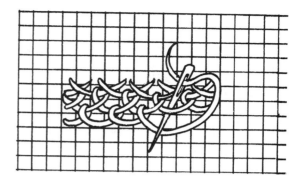

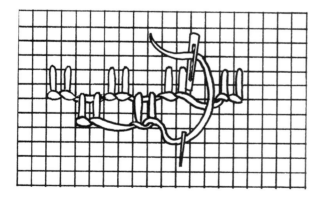

Buttonhole Filling — Spaced

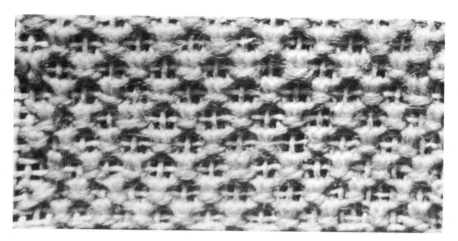

Buttonhole, Tailor's

This is similar to the stitch in diagram A, but it has an extra loop twisted round the needle, and this forms a stronger, double-knotted edge. When the point of the needle protrudes at the lower edge of the stitch, over the working yarn, it is necessary to hold this yarn near the eye of the needle and pass it under the point of the needle from right to left, before pulling the needle through.

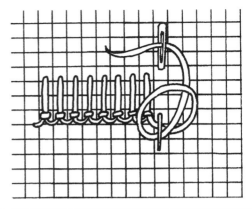

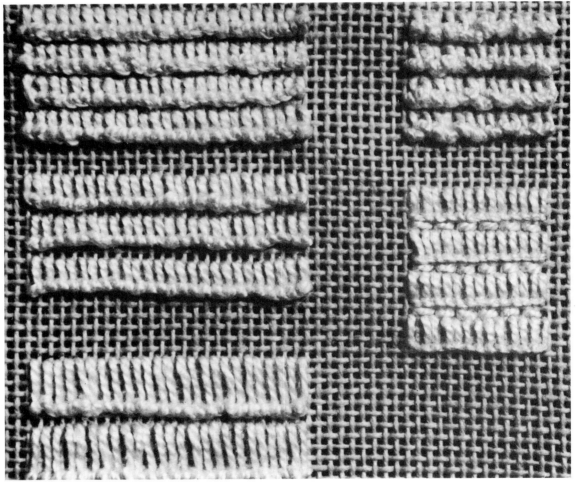

Buttonhole Wheels

These are very freely worked in simple Buttonhole Stitch. The inner wheel, which is worked first, has all the stitches radiating from the centre. The outer ring is then put in around this inner wheel, with care being taken to see that these stitches also radiate from the centre.

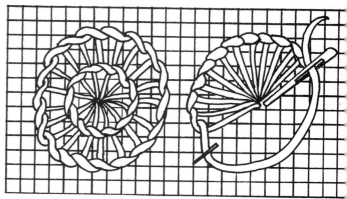

Byzantine

This stitch is worked diagonally over four inter-sections of the canvas and four horizontal threads, and it is used for covering large areas of canvas with a pattern of stitches, arranged to give a 'stepped' effect. The diagram shows how compensation stitches of different sizes are needed to complete the pattern within a rectangular area.

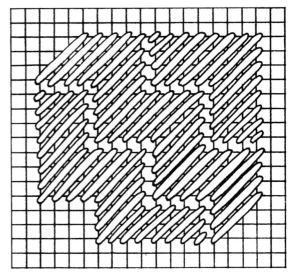

Captive Rice

This stitch consists of a Rice Stitch which is surrounded on all four sides by groups of three straight stitches, worked over four, six and eight threads of the canvas respectively. The one thread, which is left between the blocks of straight stitches, can either remain unworked, as in the diagram, or a tiny cross stitch can be worked over it. The resultant effect is of an attractive stitch with the appearance of a four-petalled flower.

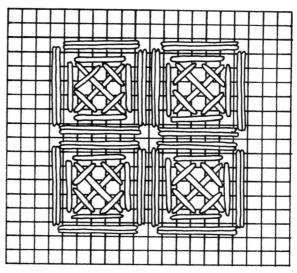

Cashmere

This stitch, which is a useful one for covering large areas of background, consists of a series of groups of diagonal stitches. Each group contains three stitches, which, when being worked from left to right, all start immediately beneath one another, one over one intersection of the canvas and two over two intersections. As it is usual to begin working at the top left-hand corner of the area to be covered, and to proceed diagonally downwards, each unit of three stitches will commence one thread of the canvas to the right of the point where the last stitch in the previous unit began.

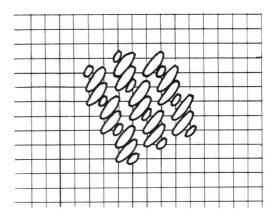

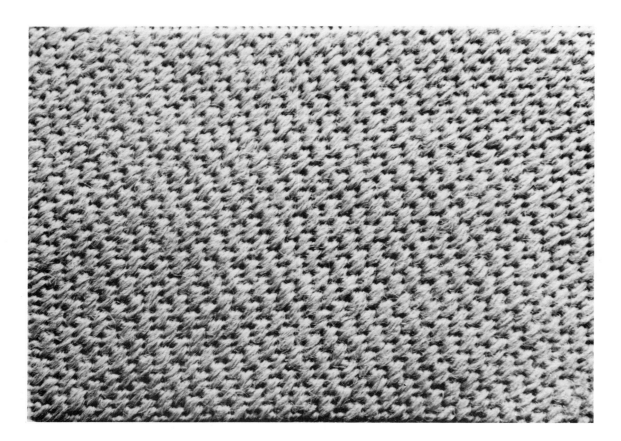

Cashmere — Straight

This straight version of Cashmere Stitch consists of units of four diagonal stitches, one over one intersection of the canvas, followed by two over two intersections, followed by another one over one intersection. These units are generally worked in rows horizontally, starting at the top left-hand corner of the area to be covered.

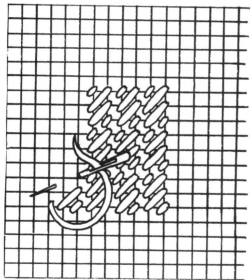

Chain, Broad

Can be worked over any number of canvas threads and in any direction

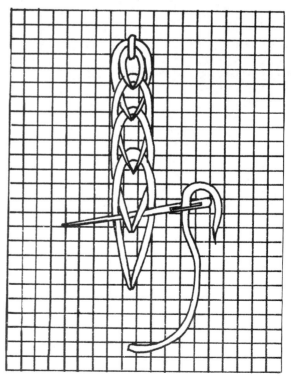

Caterpillar. See Bullion

Chain — Continuous

This stitch is started at the top of the work and
proceeds straight downwards. When the working
yarn is brought up through the canvas, it is held
with the left thumb in a small loop on the canvas,
whilst the needle is taken back down again
through the same hole from which it has just
emerged and is brought up two or more horizontal
threads of the canvas down and taken through the
loop, ready to begin the next stitch.

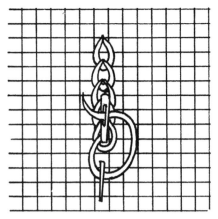

Chain — Detached

In this version of Chain Stitch each individual stitch is separated from the others. A row of these stitches is worked from left to right across the canvas, beginning with a first stitch worked as in the continuous version above. When, however, the needle has been brought up through the loop of the working yarn to complete the stitch, it is taken down again over one horizontal thread of the canvas into the hole immediately below, and thus it ties the loop down. The second stitch in the row is started two vertical threads of the canvas to the right of the first one, and all the other stitches in the row are worked with the same interval between them. Each stitch in the second row is placed to begin in the empty hole between the tie-down stitches in the first row.

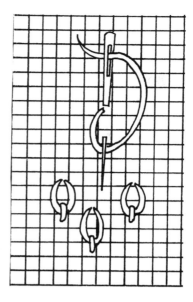

Chain, Detached — Half-drop

This half-drop version of Detached Chain Stitch
is worked in very much the same way as the simple
detached version, but a space of four vertical
threads of the canvas is left between individual
stitches in a row, when they are worked horizontally across the canvas, and the stitches in the
following row fit exactly between them, with a
drop of half the length of a stitch. This version of
the stitch is excellent for the way in which it
covers the canvas.

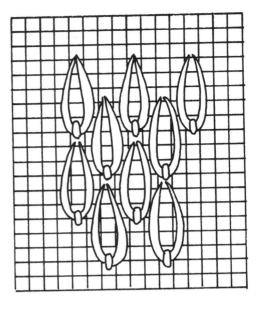

Chain, Detached Eye

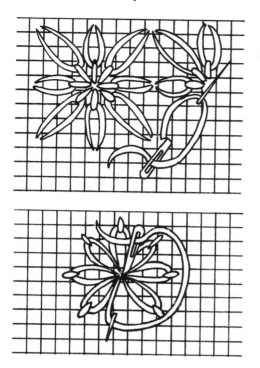

Chain, Long-tailed

This version of Detached Chain Stitch is very good as an attractive filling stitch. It is started at the top left-hand corner of the area to be covered and is worked diagonally down across the canvas to the right. The main element of the stitch is worked over two horizontal threads of the canvas, with the tying-down stitch taken down over six horizontal threads. The next stitch is dropped down two horizontal threads and one vertical thread to the right.

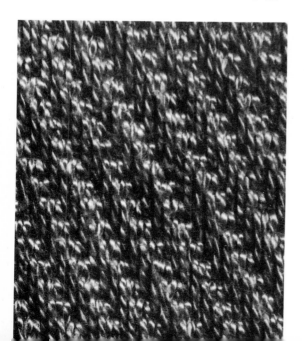

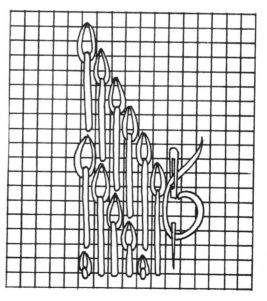

Chain — Twisted

This version of the stitch is worked in a way which is similar to that for Continuous Chain Stitch, but, when the needle has been brought up to begin the stitch, it does not go back into the same hole from which it emerged, but is taken into the hole which is one vertical thread of the canvas to the left and is brought up again two or more horizontal threads immediately below the hole from which the stitch began and through the loop of the working yarn as before.

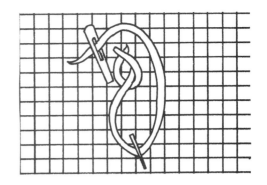

Chained Cross. See Cross, Chained

Chained Cross — Variation. See Cross, Chained—Variation

Chequer

This stitch is formed by alternating squares of Tent Stitch and Cushion Stitch. Each square is worked over four vertical and four horizontal threads of the canvas. The squares of Tent Stitch each contain sixteen stitches, and the Cushion Stitches are in the form of squares of seven diagonal straight stitches arranged in graduated lengths of from one to four intersections of the canvas.

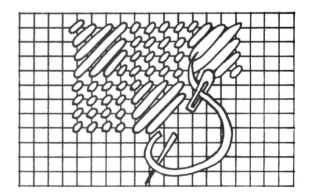

Chessboard

Groups of four vertical stitches over four horizontal threads of the canvas are worked in a chessboard pattern. Each group has a large cross stitch worked over it, which extends from corner to corner and covers four horizontal and three vertical threads of the canvas. This cross stitch is held down in the middle by means of a small horizontal stitch. In the spaces left between these groups of stitches other groups, consisting solely of the four vertical stitches over four horizontal threads of the canvas, are then worked.

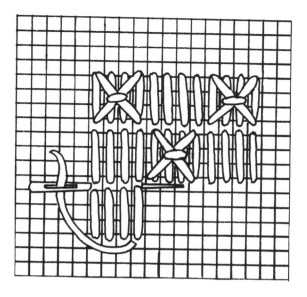

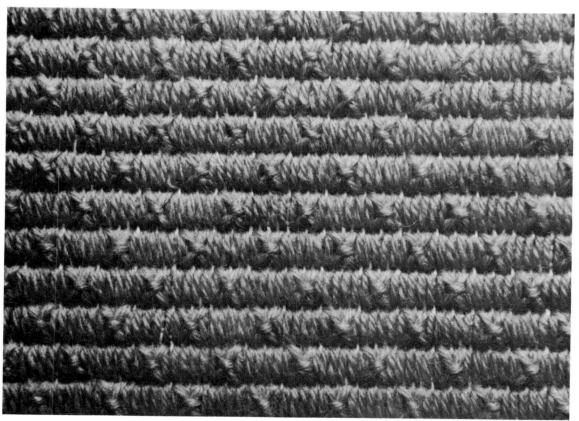

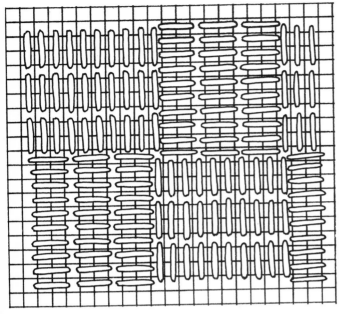

Chessboard Filling

In working this stitch a larger chessboard pattern is built up of rectangular groups of vertical and horizontal stitches, as shown in the diagram. The individual stitches are worked over three threads of the canvas, and each rectangular group of stitches is composed of three rows of ten individual stitches, with alternate groups containing only vertical stitches, and the other groups being made up entirely of horizontal stitches.

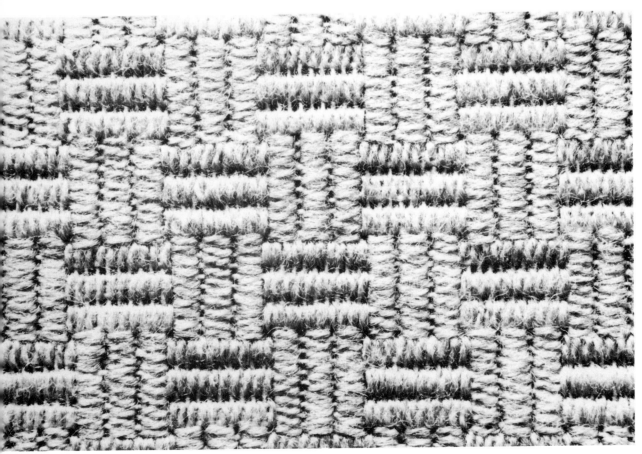

Chinese. See Pekinese

Circular Eye. See Eye, Circular

Close Cover

In working this tiny stitch the yarn is taken up over two horizontal and one vertical thread of the canvas to the right of the point from which it emerged. The needle is then brought up again two vertical threads of the canvas to the right of the point where the first stitch was started and it goes down again into the same hole in the canvas as the first stitch thus forming an inverted V-shape. Rows of these stitches are worked, and finally a series of back stitches over two vertical threads of the canvas is put in between the rows.

This stitch can be worked larger, by altering the number of horizontal threads of the canvas it is worked over: diagram A shows it worked over two horizontal threads and photograph B over three.

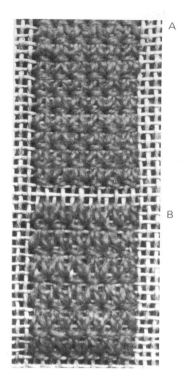

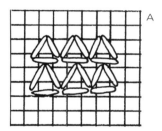

Compact Filling

This stitch can be worked in rows from left to right either horizontally across the canvas, or diagonally downwards. The yarn is brought up through the canvas three vertical threads to the right of the top left-hand corner of the area to be covered, and a stitch is taken down over three horizontal threads of the canvas. The needle is then brought up three vertical threads to the left, and a stitch is taken back over these three threads and down into the same hole at the base of the first stitch. Two oblique stitches, each one over two intersections of the canvas, are then put in one beside the other in a position immediately beneath the right angle formed by the first two stitches. If this stitch is being worked in rows horizontally across the canvas, a space of five vertical threads of the canvas should be left between the groups of stitches. The diagram shows clearly the position of subsequent rows of stitches.

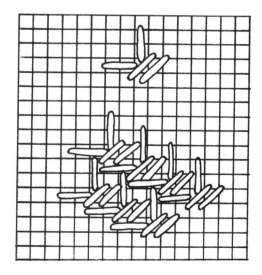

Work this stitch from left to right then repeat dropping down one horizontal and two vertical threads to the right

Worked in wool

Worked in cotton

Continental. See Tent

Coral Knot (Also known as Snail's Trail)

This stitch is worked from right to left, the yarn being brought up for the start of the first stitch at a point one horizontal thread of canvas down from the top right-hand corner of the area to be covered. The needle is then taken down through the canvas one horizontal thread above this point and is brought out again one horizontal thread down and three vertical threads to the left, being passed through the loop of the working yarn to make the knot, as shown in the diagram. The spacing of the knots can be varied to suit the shape of the area which is being worked.

Although this is generally thought of as a crewel work stitch, it can be used quite well on canvas, not only as a filling stitch, but also for the working of outlines.

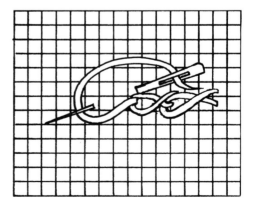

When this stitch is worked in a zigzag, it is known as Knotted Zigzag Stitch.

Coral Zigzag. See Knotted Zigzag

Cornered Chain

A series of vertical straight stitches over four horizontal threads of the canvas are first worked in rows horizontally across the area to be covered. The individual stitches, which are separated from one another by four vertical threads of the canvas, should be quite tightly tensioned. The yarn is then brought out at the top left-hand corner of the area being worked, and it is looped loosely over and back under the first vertical stitch to its right, before being taken down again into the same hole in the canvas, from which it emerged.

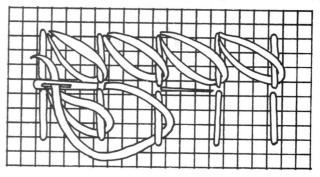

Work straight stitches first and pull tightly. The loop should be tensioned loosely

Cretan

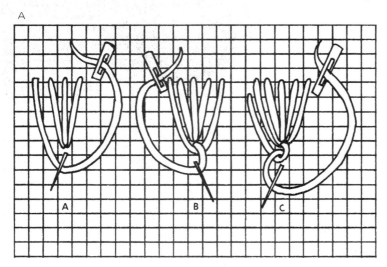

This stitch can be worked both as a filling stitch and as a border stitch. It is started by taking a straight stitch down over five horizontal threads of the canvas. Then two other straight stitches are put in, one on either side of this first stitch and starting one thread of the canvas either to the left or to the right of the first stitch, but both going down into the same hole as this first stitch. The needle is then brought out again on the top line, but one vertical thread of the canvas to the left, and is taken down on the opposite side of the group of three stitches one vertical thread to the right. The working yarn is left slack in a loop, and the needle is brought up through the hole in the canvas where the group of three stitches were taken down, and also through the loop of yarn. After this process of starting the stitch has been completed, an oblique straight stitch is put in first on one side and then on the other, the needle being taken down one horizontal thread below the beginning of the last stitch on the left and brought up one horizontal thread below the end of the last stitch in the centre and through the loop of the working yarn, and again being taken one horizontal thread down on the right and brought up in the same hole in the centre and through the loop of the yarn. This process is then continued, as shown in the diagram, to form a vertical row of stitches, and other similar rows of stitches are worked to cover the area required.

It is also possible to work this stitch in a freer, expanding manner, when it can be useful in working shapes such as leaves. In addition it may be worked diagonally, as is clearly shown in diagram B.

A

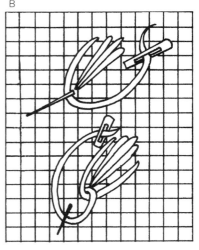

B

Cretan Border

A long straight stitch is taken horizontally from
left to right over six vertical threads of the canvas.
The needle is then brought up again through the
same hole in the canvas from which the first
stitch started, and it is taken down four vertical
threads to the right, tying down the first straight
stitch at the same time. It is then brought up
once more at a point level with the right-hand
end of the first long stitch, but one horizontal
thread of the canvas down. To complete this
third stitch, the needle is taken down at a point
four vertical threads of the canvas to the left
and one horizontal thread up, so that the working
yarn holds the second stitch down. The needle is
then brought up again two vertical threads of the
canvas to the left, at a point immediately beneath
the hole where the first two stitches were started.
From this point it is possible to repeat the process,
as shown in the diagram. The diagram below
shows clearly how to work this stitch diagonally.

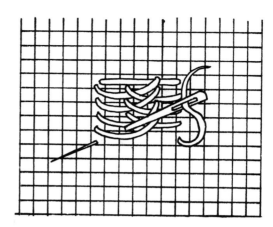

Cretan Border, Diagonal

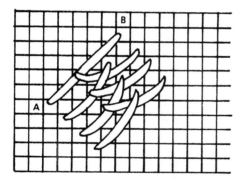

Cretan — Variation

This stitch is similar in appearance to ordinary Cretan Stitch, but the individual stitches are tied down instead of being knotted, as in the usual form of the stitch, and this gives it a very neat and much flatter appearance. It starts with a tiny stitch over just one vertical thread of the canvas, which is tied down by means of two small vertical stitches over one horizontal thread, which are worked one on each side of the centre vertical thread. The second stitch is similar, but slightly larger, being worked from a point one vertical thread to the left of the first stitch to a point one vertical thread to the right of the first stitch. The yarn is left in a slight loop, as shown in the diagram, so that it can be tied down, as was done in the first stitch, by two small vertical stitches over one horizontal thread, placed one on each side of the centre vertical thread and one hori-

zontal thread immediately beneath those in the first stitch. The third stitch starts with the yarn being brought up one vertical thread to the left of the second stitch and is taken down three vertical threads to the right and three horizontal threads down. A small vertical stitch over one horizontal thread of the canvas then ties it down at a point one horizontal thread immediately below the similar stitch in the row above. The fourth stitch is taken from a point one vertical thread to the right of the second stitch to a point three horizontal threads down and three vertical threads back to the left, so that it crosses over the end of the third stitch, and it is tied down, as was the previous stitch, by means of a small vertical stitch over one horizontal thread of the canvas, placed immediately below the similar stitch in the row above. The process is continued in this way, as shown in the diagram.

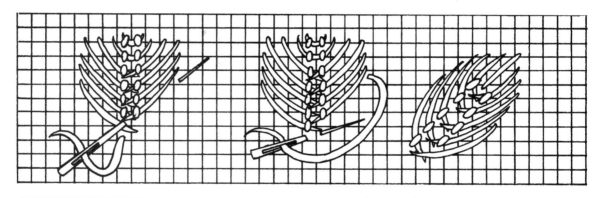

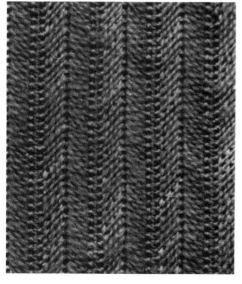

Criss-cross

This is a complicated stitch, but, as the photograph shows, it gives a very interesting texture. Each stitch is over ten horizontal and twelve vertical threads of the canvas, and the work proceeds from left to right across the area to be covered. Five of the nine individual stitches in each group radiate from the bottom left-hand corner of the stitch and four from the bottom right-hand corner. These individual stitches begin with one from the left-hand corner, followed by one from the right-hand corner, and they alternate in this way from left to right, until finally stitch number nine is taken from the bottom left-hand corner over the full width of the stitch. The diagram shows exactly where the individual stitches have to be placed.

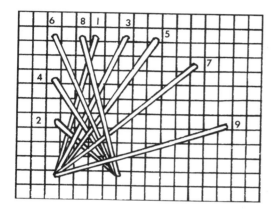

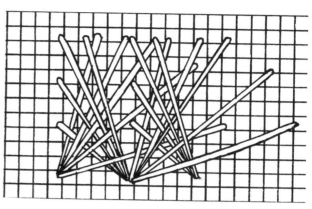

Cross

This stitch consists of two diagonal straight stitches, each over two intersections of the canvas, which cross one another at right angles. The upper stitch of each cross must always be made in the same direction, and it is the normal practice to work it from bottom left to top right of each Cross Stitch. The best effect is obtained with this stitch, if each individual cross is completed before the next one is started.

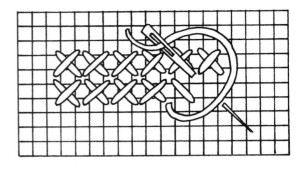

Cross, Broad. See Broad Cross

Cross, Chained

A normal Cross Stitch is worked over four intersections of the canvas. Then the needle is brought up one horizontal thread of the canvas directly below the top right-hand corner of the cross. The working yarn is placed in a loop, as shown in the diagram, and is held in position over the Cross Stitch, whilst the needle is taken down into the hole in the canvas which is two horizontal threads below the hole from which the yarn emerged, and it is brought up once more three vertical threads to the left and one horizontal thread above this point. The needle is then taken over the loop of the yarn and down into the hole which is one intersection of the canvas up to the left. This holds the loop in position, and work can proceed with the next stitch.

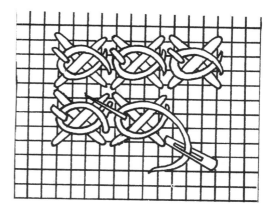

Cross Chained — Variation

In this version of Chained Cross Stitch the working is exactly the same as that for normal Chained Cross, except that, after the loop of yarn has been placed in position above the cross, the needle is merely slipped underneath the whole stitch and brought up through the loop, without being taken down through the canvas. The final stitch to hold down the loop of yarn before proceeding to the next stitch, remains the same as before.

There is very little difference in appearance between this Variation and normal Chained Cross Stitch, but while the Variation is quite suitable for using on wall-panels and pictures, or anywhere else where it will not be subjected to hard wear, normal Chained Cross Stitch is the correct stitch to use on chair-seats and stool-tops.

Cross, Diagonal

This stitch consists of an Upright Cross Stitch, worked over four vertical and four horizontal threads of the canvas, with a single diagonal stitch taken from the hole at the base of the cross into the hole at the right-hand end of the horizontal stitch, as shown in the diagram.

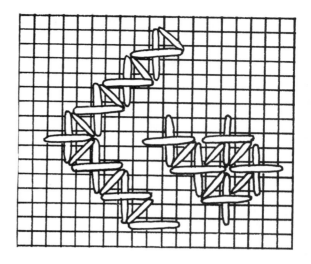

Cross, Double. See Double Cross

Cross, Double Plaited. See Double Cross Plaited

Cross, Interlaced. See Interlaced Cross

Cross, Oblong

This is a Cross Stitch which can be worked over
four, six or more even numbers of horizontal
threads of the canvas and one or two vertical
threads. It can be worked in horizontal rows
across the canvas, or it can be used to form a
half-drop pattern, when the crosses are placed
in rows diagonally. The tension of the work is
always improved, if each cross is completed
before gong on to the next.

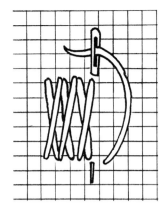

Cross, Oblong — Double-tied

An Oblong Cross is taken over seven horizontal
and two vertical threads of the canvas, and it is
tied down across the centre with two horizontal
back stitches over two vertical threads, one placed
above the other.

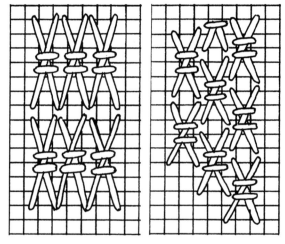

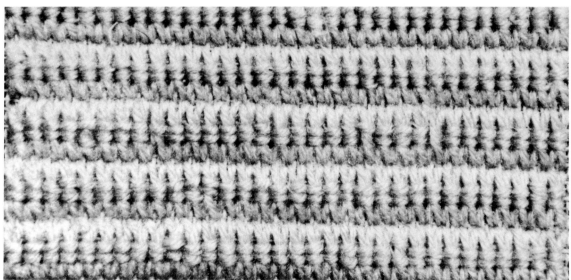

Cross, Oblong — Encroaching

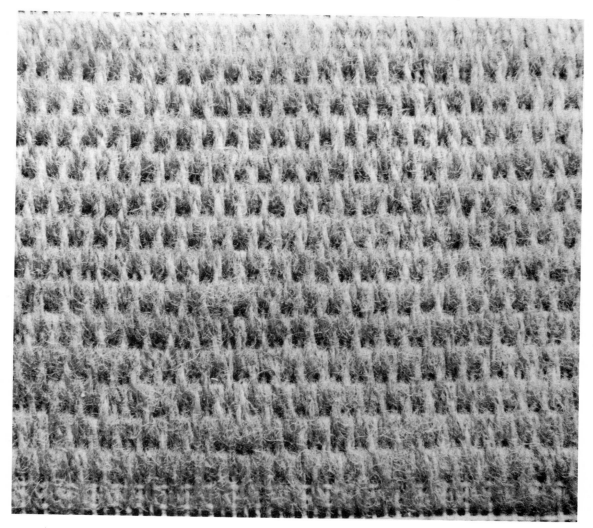

Cross, Oblong — Horizontal

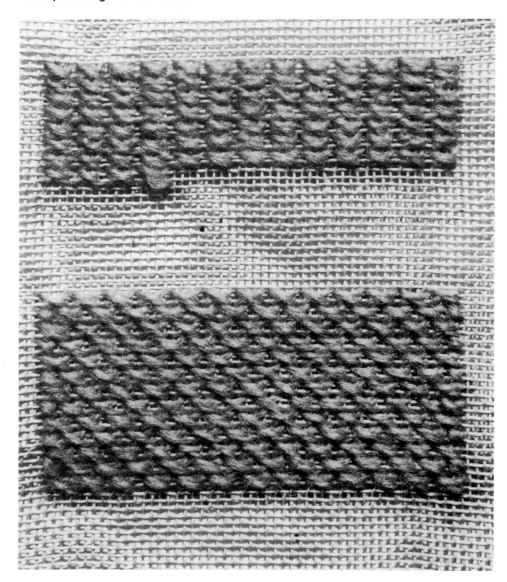

Worked over four vertical and two horizontal threads
of the canvas

Cross, Oblong Overlaid

In this variation of Oblong Cross the initial horizontal rows of crosses are worked over six horizontal and two vertical threads of the canvas. Then further horizontal rows of crosses of the same size are worked across them by starting three horizontal threads of the canvas down in the space left between stitches in the original rows. This overstitch can, of course, be worked in a different colour or weight of yarn, if so desired.

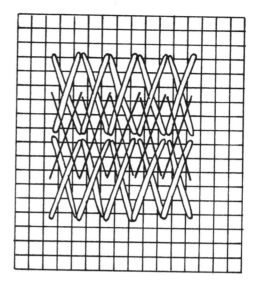

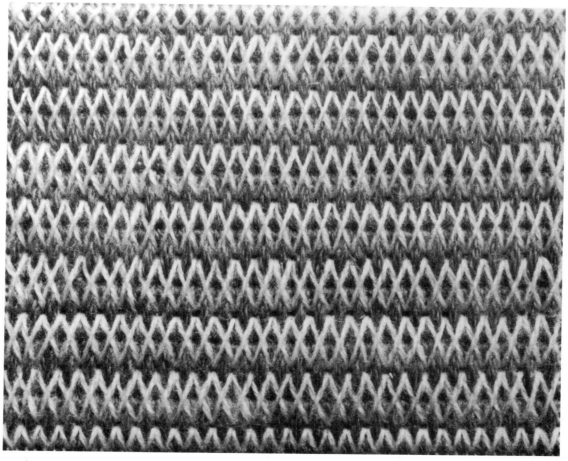

Cross, Oblong with small cross

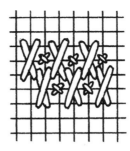

Cross Plus Two

This is a very attractive stitch, which, when it is worked with a fine, tightly spun wool or pearl cotton, gives a lace-like appearance to the embroidery. A Cross Stitch is worked over six horizontal and four vertical threads of the canvas. One vertical straight stitch over six horizontal threads is then taken over the centre of the cross, and one horizontal straight stitch is worked across the base of the cross. Subsequent rows are worked with a half-drop from the row above.

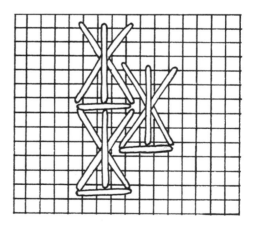

Worked with a fine wool

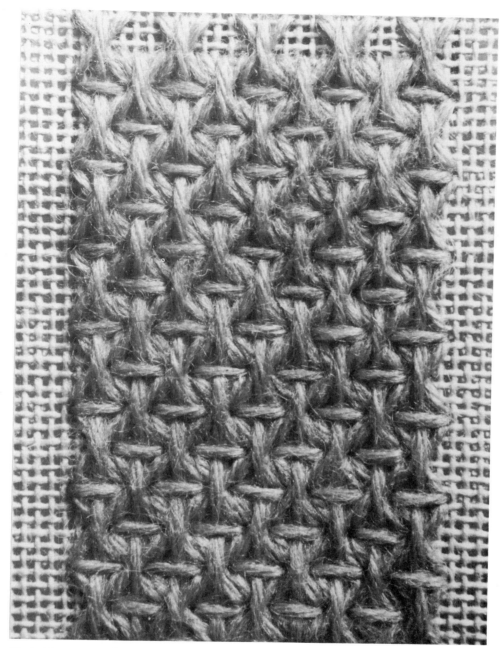

Worked in coarse wool

Cross, Swedish. See Swedish Cross

Cross, Triple. See Triple Cross

Cross, Triple Encroaching. See Triple
Cross Encroaching

Cross, Upright
(Also known as Straight Cross)

In this version of Cross Stitch one vertical stitch over two horizontal threads of the canvas is crossed by one horizontal stitch over two vertical threads. The second row of crosses is worked in between those in the first row, so that the rows interlock, and individual stitches of four adjacent crosses all go into the same hole in the canvas. This stitch is also sometimes called Straight Cross Stitch.

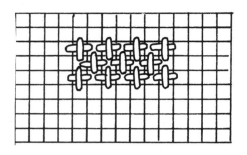

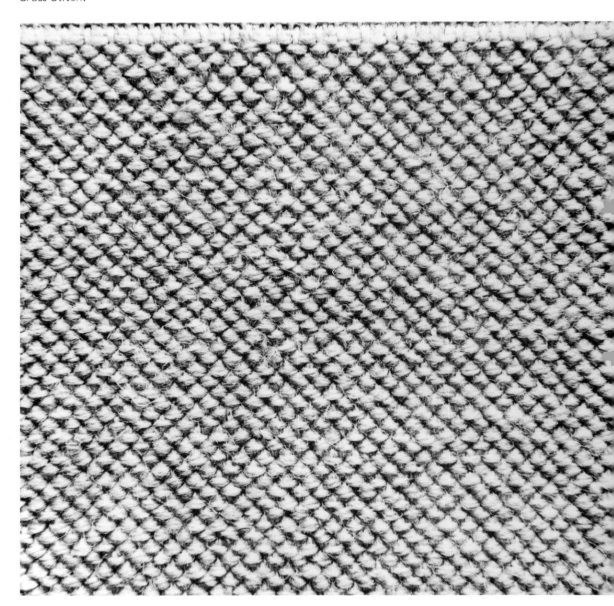

Crossed — Cornered Cushion. See Cushion
Crossed — Cornered

Crossed Corners. See Rice

Crow's-foot

Three individual straight stitches, all radiating from a central hole at the base of the crow's-foot, are worked over three horizontal threads of the canvas. The centre stitch is a vertical stitch over three horizontal threads, and those on either side are oblique stitches over three horizontal and two vertical threads of the canvas. A single vertical straight stitch, worked over three horizontal threads, separates these groups. The horizontal back stitch over four vertical threads of the canvas, which is placed between groups of stitches in successive rows, is perhaps easier to put in after all the rows have been worked.

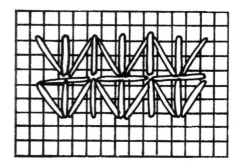

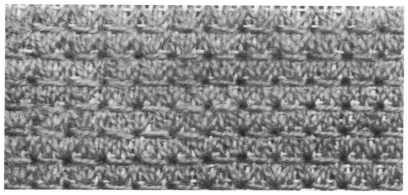

over three threads

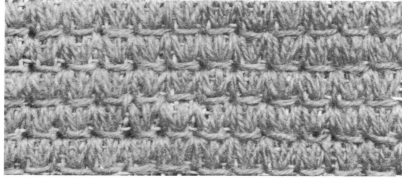

over four threads

Curtain

This is a square stitch over eight threads of the canvas. The basis of it is a Cushion Stitch, over which eight vertical straight stitches are worked to extend across the full height of the cushion. These superimposed stitches are divided into two groups of four, the left-hand group being drawn back to the left and held in position by means of a stitch, which is brought up through the canvas at a point four threads down on the left-hand side of the cushion, is carried under the four vertical stitches in question, is then brought back over them to the left and is taken down again into the hole from which it emerged. The right-hand group of vertical stitches is drawn back and held in the same way to the right. The direction of the diagonal stitches in a row of the basic Cushion Stitches alternates between being taken from bottom left to top right and from top left to bottom right of the square.

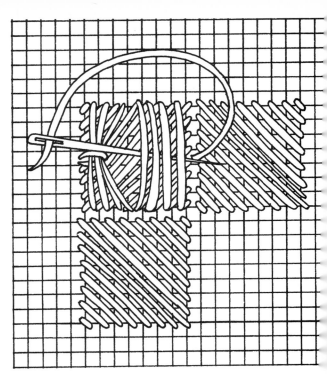

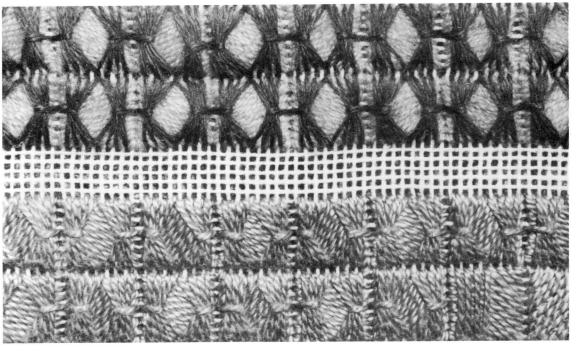

Cushion (Also known as Scottish)

This is a square stitch in which an uneven number of individual diagonal stitches — usually five or seven — is worked to form a square. A set of five such diagonal stitches, for example, would be worked over a sequence of one, two, three, two and one intersections of the canvas. The cushions are worked in rows horizontally, and each cushion is completely surrounded by a row of Tent Stitch. All the stitches should slant in the same direction. A pleasing effect is obtained, if a contrasting yarn is used to work the Tent Stitch: this could be a contrast either in colour or in type of fibre.

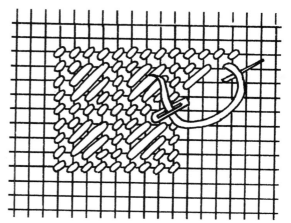

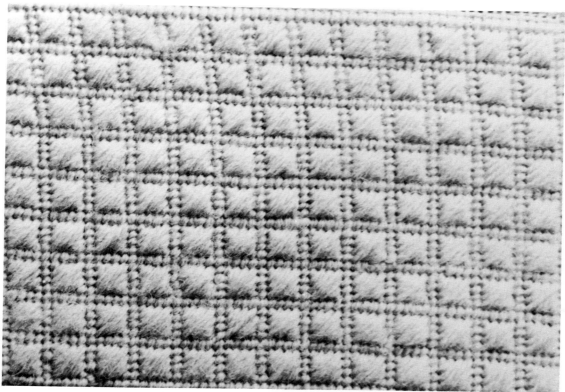

Cushion Crossed-cornered

This is a most attractive stitch, especially when it is worked quite large. Four large cushion stitches are worked to form a square, as shown in the diagram. In the top right-hand cushion and the bottom left-hand one the diagonal stitches, with which they are constructed, follow the diagonal of the large square from bottom left to top right, and in the other two cushions they are worked in the opposite direction. Then one corner of each cushion stitch is overworked with a contrasting yarn. This stitch is excellent for covering large areas of canvas, where the size of the large squares can be varied.

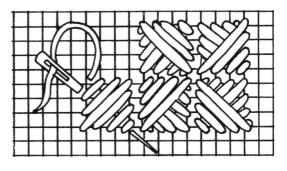

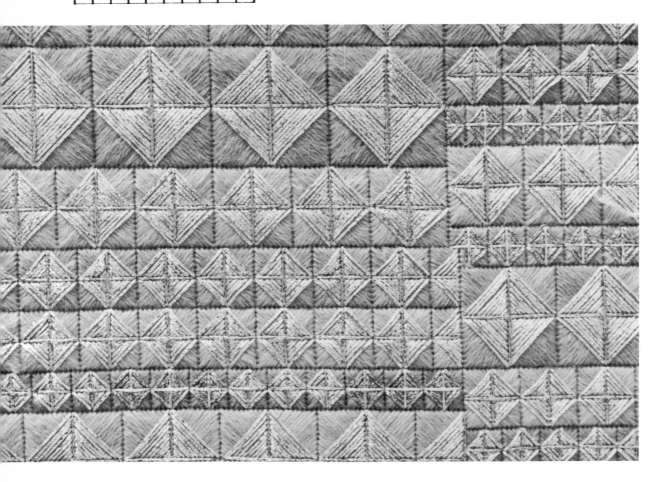

Cushion — Straight

Six vertical straight stitches are worked over one, three, five, five, three and one horizontal threads of the canvas. When the second row is worked, the groups of stitches fit together, with the short ones over one horizontal thread of the canvas fitting in immediately below the long stitches over five threads in the previous row.

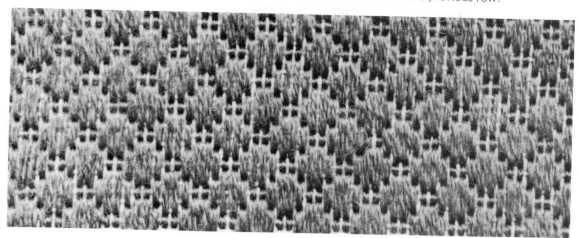

Cushion — Variation

An attractive variation of Cushion Stitch is obtained by working the stitch as in the diagram, where the direction of the diagonal stitches alternates from square to square, and the Tent Stitch is omitted.

Cushion — Variation, Reversed

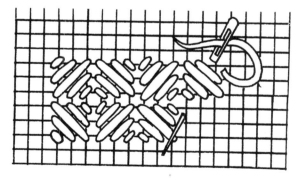

Damask

This stitch is worked diagonally over four horizontal and four vertical threads of the canvas, and it gives an open effect to the finished embroidery. To start working the stitch, the needle should be brought up through the canvas at a point eight horizontal threads down from the top left-hand corner of the area to be covered and four vertical threads to the right. A diagonal stitch is taken from this point upwards to the left over four intersections of the canvas, and the needle is brought out again six vertical threads back to the right and two horizontal threads down. The second stitch is then put in, also over four intersections of the canvas, in a position parallel to the first stitch, and then a third stitch parallel to the second. In this way an oblique row of diagonal stitches is worked across the canvas, and similarly a second row is put in by starting from a point six horizontal threads of the canvas below the first stitch in the first row. After this pattern of stitches has been worked over the required area, another set of smaller diagonal stitches, each one over two intersections of the canvas, is put in between the original large stitches. These stitches can be worked either with the same weight of yarn as the first stitches, or, as in the photograph, with a much thinner yarn and one of a different colour.

The diagram also shows the compensating stitches, which need to be put in at the top and bottom of a rectangular area and down the sides.

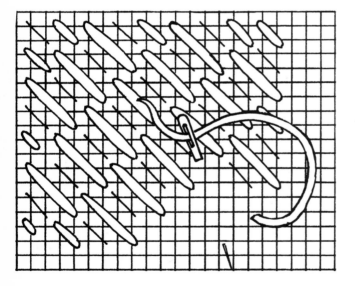

Damask Darning 1

Two horizontal stitches are worked, one under the other, over four vertical threads of the canvas, and a row of these stitches is put in across the area to be covered. In the second row the stitches are placed so that they begin two vertical threads in from the beginning of the first row, and in the third row they begin immediately beneath the first stitches in the first row, so that a brick pattern is produced.

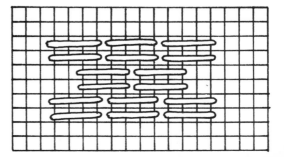

Damask Darning 2

This version of Damask Darning Stitch is commenced in the same way as the original simple version shown above with a row of groups of two horizontal straight stitches, worked over four vertical threads of the canvas, but one vertical thread is left unworked between each of the groups of two straight stitches, and this is later covered by a Cross Stitch. The second row consists of groups of two horizontal straight stitches over two vertical threads of the canvas, alternating with groups of similar stitches over three vertical threads. These groups are placed so that those over two vertical threads of the canvas lie immediately beneath the centre of the groups of two

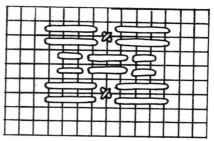

horizontal straight stitches in the first row, and the groups over three vertical threads lie immediately beneath the cross stitches. This pattern is then repeated in subsequent rows, as is shown in the diagram.

Detached Chain. See Chain, Detached

Detached Chain Eye. See Chain, Detached Eye

Detached Chain Half-drop. See Chain, Detached — Half drop

Diagonal Cross. See Cross, Diagonal

Diagonal Double Dutch. See Dutch, Double Diagonal

Diagonal — Large

This is a very good stitch for filling large areas of background. In this larger form the stitch is constructed of four individual diagonal stitches, worked over one, two, three and two intersections of the canvas respectively. See the diagram. If, however, a fine mesh canvas (18 or finer) is being used, it might prove better if the individual stitches were worked over two, three, four and three intersections of the canvas. Subsequent rows of the stitch fit into the line of stitches in the previous row, the largest ones always coming into line diagonally with the smallest ones in the previous row.

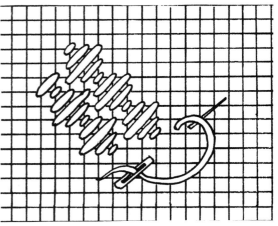

Diagonal Leaf. See Leaf Diagonal

Diagonal — Small (Sometimes known as Diagonal Parisian Stitch)

The smaller version of this stitch consists of one diagonal stitch over one intersection of the canvas, followed by one over two intersections. This sequence is repeated along a diagonal of the canvas, starting either from the left or from the right, with subsequent rows fitting in beside one another.

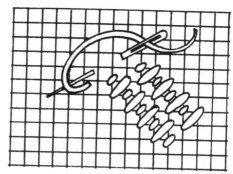

Diamond, Double — Straight. See Double Diamond — Straight

Diamond Eye

This eye stitch is formed by working over ten horizontal and ten vertical threads of the canvas. To begin the stitch the needle should be brought up at one of the corners of the diamond shape and should be taken down again over five horizontal or five vertical threads of the canvas into the centre hole. The other individual stitches are then worked by bringing the needle up from each hole in turn around the perimeter of the diamond shape and taking it down each time into the centre hole of the diamond. As this centre hole is such an essential feature of all eye stitches, it is necessary to work with a yarn that will keep it from becoming clogged in any way. A fine, tightly spun, non-hairy type of wool is good for this purpose, or a pearl cotton, which always looks very attractive, as it tends to have more pull than wool, and this fact helps to keep the centre hole clear.

Diamond Eyelet with Straight Stitches

Detail of **The Bare Mountain** designed by Mary Rhodes and
worked by Joan Guest
(Size: approx. 84 cm x 38 cm – 33 in. x 15 in.)
This panel is based on a design in which three horizontal,
curved lines and two circular shapes are used, with thin,
wedge-shaped areas of a darker colour cutting across them,
to suggest a range of mountains. The yellow sky is worked in
Hungarian Stitch, heavily flecked in places with a single
strand of black cotton. The numerous stitches used to work
this panel, which include not only Hungarian, but also
Cashmere, Milanese and Half-Rhodes, can all be found in
the dictionary. The canvas used was 16 mesh, single thread
canvas.

Sunflowers worked by Tina Palmer
(Size: approx. 53.5 cm square – 21 in. square)
A beautifully worked panel of stylized sunflowers, the
centres of which have been very successfully rendered
entirely in Stem Stitch and French Knots. The petals have a
line of Portuguese Stem Stitch down the centre of each one,
and the rest of the petal is worked in Small Diagonal Stitch
with an outline of Tent Stitch. Rhodes, Smyrna and Upright
Cross Stitch have been used for the leaves, and a
background of Hungarian Stitch completes the picture.
The canvas is 16 mesh, single thread canvas.

Diamond Straight

This is one of the old, attractive stitches, which is seldom seen in these days. The basic element is a diamond shape, formed by placing side by side five upright straight stitches, which pass over one, three, five, three and one horizontal threads of the canvas respectively. The diamond shapes are surrounded by small, vertical straight stitches over one horizontal thread of the canvas, and they form an attractive pattern, as shown in the diagram.

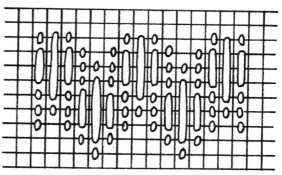

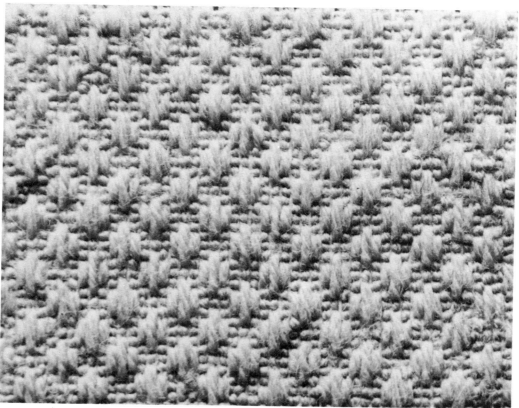

Double Cross

A cross is formed by working two horizontal stitches side by side over seven vertical threads of the canvas and crossing them with two vertical stitches over seven horizontal threads. This double cross is itself crossed diagonally from bottom left to top right by the working of two stitches side by side over six intersections of the canvas, and then from bottom right to top left by two similar diagonal stitches over six intersections. A small upright cross stitch is worked over the two threads left between the four groups of double cross stitches, which are also separated from one another by the working of a horizontal or a vertical stitch over five threads of the canvas.

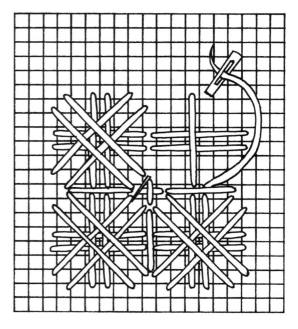

Double Cross Plaited

This variant form of Double Cross Stitch is obtained by the individual stitches being plaited over and under one another. The method of working is shown clearly in the numbered diagram. The final stitch, which is number eight, is slipped under stitch number five.

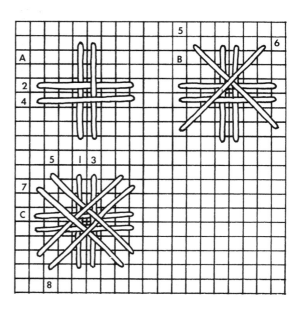

Double Diamond — Straight

In this stitch six vertical straight stitches are worked over one, three, five, five, three and one horizontal threads of the canvas respectively. The sequence is repeated straight across the area to be covered, and subsequent rows of the stitch fit in together, with the two long stitches being worked immediately beneath the small stitches in the previous row.

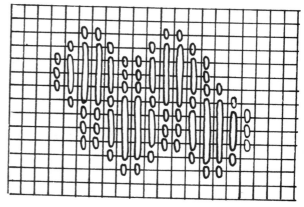

Double Knot

The size of the knot in this stitch will depend upon the thickness of the yarn used. The stitch should be started by working a Twisted Chain Stitch, as shown at A in the diagram. The needle is then taken under the loop of the chain from right to left (B), and the yarn is taken right round the base of the stitch (C), so that the needle can pass under the lower limb of the chain and over its upper limb. Once more the yarn is taken right round the stitch, and the needle is put into the canvas just one hole to the left of the point where the initial stitch was begun. It should then be brought out again at the base of the stitch and should be taken through the final loop which has been formed (D). It is advisable at this stage to insert the needle under the middle section of the knot to hold it up before the loop of the yarn is tightened.

This Double Knot Stitch can be worked either as a continuous row of stitches, or as separate units.

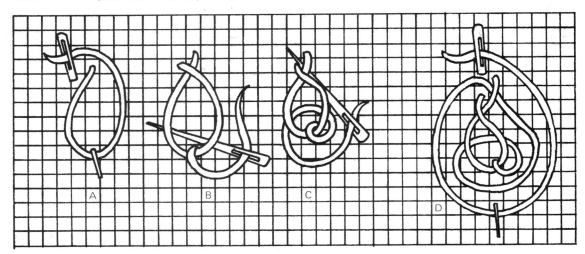

Top two rows worked in wool, bottom two rows worked in a strand of the canvas

Dutch

This stitch consists of rows of Oblong Cross Stitches, worked horizontally over four vertical and two horizontal threads of the canvas, with an over-stitching of vertical straight stitches, each one over four horizontal threads. The rows of oblong crosses are worked first and are fitted neatly into one another, as shown in the diagram. Then for the over-stitching the needle is brought out one horizontal thread above the centre of each cross, and the yarn is taken down over four horizontal threads. A strand of silk or of finely spun wool is very suitable for the over-sewing, as it will not obscure the oblong crosses beneath it.

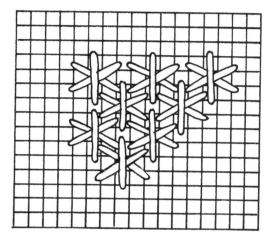

Dutch Double

This stitch is worked vertically downwards over
the canvas. The first stitch consists of an oblong
cross, worked over four vertical and two horizontal threads of the canvas, which is tied down
by a vertical stitch over three horizontal threads
of the canvas. An oblong cross, this time untied,
is then worked in the space beneath the first
tied cross, and the working proceeds with a tied
cross alternating with one that is untied. When the
whole area has been worked over, a back stitch
over four horizontal threads of the canvas is placed
between the vertical rows as shown in the diagram.

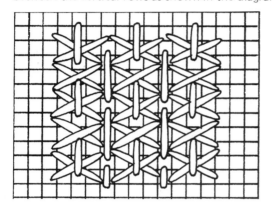

Dutch Double-Diagonal

In the diagonal version of Double Dutch Stitch,
as shown in the diagram, the oblong cross is
worked over six vertical and two horizontal
threads of the canvas, and each cross has a vertical
back stitch over three horizontal threads tying
it down, and also a back stitch, worked over two
intersections of the canvas, crosses over the ends
of the upper stitch of the oblong crosses.

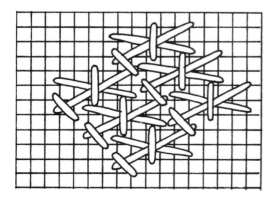

Eastern

This stitch is based on a square of two horizontal and two vertical threads of the canvas. The needle should be brought out to begin the stitch at the top left-hand corner of the square. A horizontal stitch over two threads of the canvas is then put in, and the needle is brought up again two intersections of the canvas down to the left, from which point a vertical stitch over two threads is worked, so that the needle goes down again into the same hole from which it first emerged. From here the needle is brought up at the opposite corner of the square and is taken to the left over the vertical stitch and back under it, without penetrating the canvas. It is then taken in the same way over and back under the top horizontal stitch and it finishes by being taken down into the hole at the bottom right-hand corner of the square, from which it emerged.

As the diagram shows, it is possible to work Eastern Stitch also over a square of four threads, but for this larger sized stitch a somewhat thicker yarn would be required.

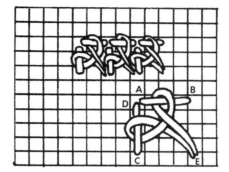

Encroaching Straight

Two vertical straight stitches over eight horizontal threads of the canvas are worked side by side at intervals across the area to be covered, leaving three vertical threads of the canvas unworked between the groups of stitches. When the second row is worked, the groups of two stitches encroach over those of the previous row by four horizontal threads. Encroaching Straight Stitch is also a form of Gobelin Encroaching.

The diagrams and photographs show how this stitch is worked and also the method of working it diagonally.

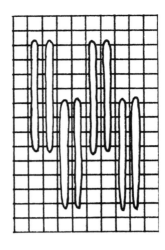

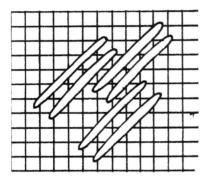

English

This is an entirely new stitch. It is worked over
six vertical and four horizontal threads of the
canvas. Five vertical straight stitches are worked
first over the four horizontal threads. The needle
is then brought up through the centre hole along
the bottom edge of the stitch and is taken down
into the centre hole on the left-hand side. It then
emerges from the centre hole on the right-hand
side, to be taken down again into the centre hole
on the bottom edge. From this point the needle
is then brought up through the centre hole on the
top edge of the stitch and taken down into the
centre hole on the left-hand side. It is brought up
once again through the centre hole on the right-
hand side and is taken down into the centre hole
at the top. A small diagonal stitch over two intersections of the canvas is then worked over each
corner of the group of vertical stitches, outside
and parallel to the four longer diagonal stitches
just worked.

The diagram and photograph also show English
Stitch worked over four horizontal and four
vertical threads of the canvas, with the second
row of the stitch dropped half-way down the
first row. Here the stitch has a basis of three
vertical straight stitches, over which one diagonal
stitch is worked across each corner.

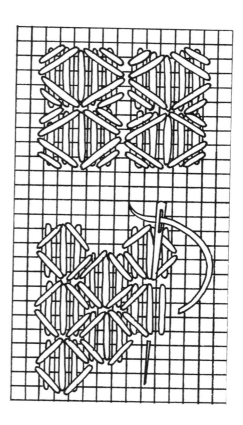

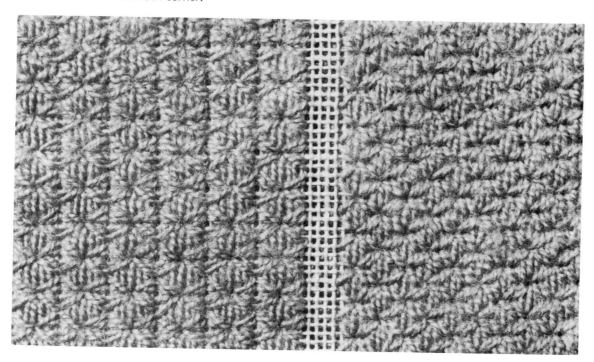

English — Diagonal

This can also be worked diagonally across the
canvas as a half-drop.

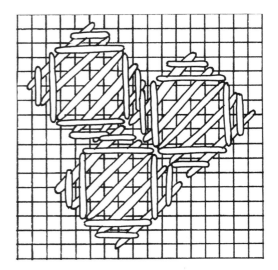

Eye, Half. See Half Eye

Eye, Octagonal. See Octagonal Eye

Eye, Woven. See Woven Eye

Eyelet

This stitch is generally worked over a square of
four threads of the canvas. From each of the
holes around the four sides of the square a stitch
is taken over two threads of the canvas and down
into the centre hole. Care must be taken, when
working such an eyelet, to arrange that the last
stitch to enter the centre hole is put in the correct
position for pulling the yarn away from the hole,
when it is being taken to the point for starting
work on the next eyelet. It is essential to do this
in order to keep the centre hole open and un-
cluttered.

Eyelet — Circular

This stitch is about as near to a circle in shape as it is possible to get on a square-mesh canvas. The eyelets, which each consist of sixteen individual stitches worked over six horizontal and six vertical threads of the canvas, all going down into a central hole, are placed side by side in rows horizontally across the canvas. The second and subsequent rows of the stitches are worked so that the individual eyelets fit into the spaces between those in the previous row.

Eyelets are best worked in a fine wool or pearl cotton, or in any other fibre which is strong enough to allow the yarn to be pulled tight, in order to open up the central hole.

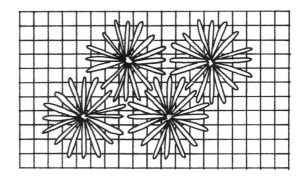

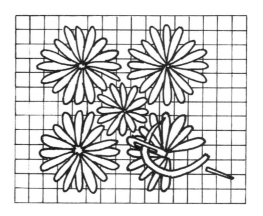

Eyelet — Circular — Variation

In this variation of the previous stitch the eyelets are placed side by side in rows both horizontally and vertically across the canvas. The intervening spaces are filled with smaller eyelets, each one consisting of twelve individual stitches, worked over two horizontal and two vertical threads of the canvas.

Fan or Ray

This square stitch is generally worked over three vertical and three horizontal threads of the canvas, but the size of the stitch can be varied. In the diagram where it is shown worked over three threads of the canvas, seven straight stitches fan out from one corner of the square into the holes along the opposite two sides. The stitch is varied by working alternate rows with the individual stitches radiating from opposite corners of the square, or by working alternate Fan Stitches in any one row so that the direction of the individual stitches is varied. See the photograph.

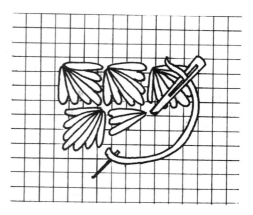

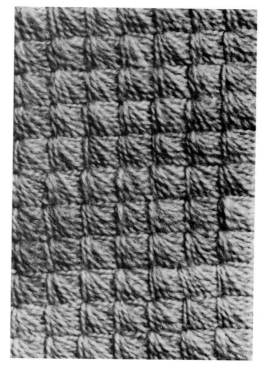

Fan Vaulting

This delightful little stitch, if worked with pearl cotton or with a fine, tightly spun wool, gives a lacy, open appearance to the embroidery. If, however, it is necessary to cover the canvas more fully, a thicker yarn may be used. The stitch consists of five individual stitches, forming a cross. Three of these stitches are over eight threads of the canvas and are worked first, the centre one of the three being a straight stitch with the other two forming a cross, which lies over the first stitch. The remaining two stitches in the group are over six threads of the canvas, and they make a final cross over all the others. In working a complete row of Fan Vaulting Stitches the crosses are placed alternately in a vertical or in a horizontal position, so that they fit neatly together, as shown in the diagram.

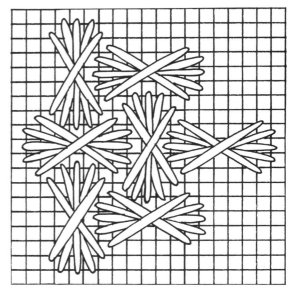

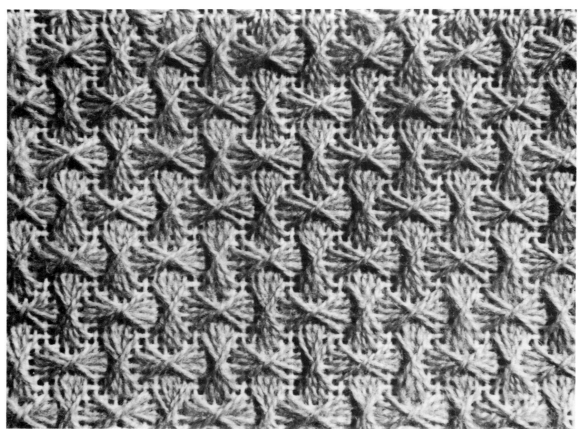

Fancy Bricking. See Bricking, Fancy

Fantail

A fan shape, covering an area of ten vertical and
five horizontal threads of the canvas, is formed by
working a total of fifteen individual stitches, whic
which are all taken from points around the cir-
cumference of the semi-circular shape and go
down into the centre hole at the base of the fan,
as shown in the diagram. Seven such individual
stitches are worked from either side of the shape,
and it is completed by the working of a central
vertical stitch over five horizontal threads of the
canvas. A small subsidiary part-eyelet stitch is
worked immediately beneath the centre of the
fan, with its central individual stitch covering
three horizontal threads of the canvas, and a back
stitch over two horizontal threads is put in immediately beneath it. The diagram shows how this is
done and how the rows of Fantail Stitch can be
fitted together to cover the canvas.

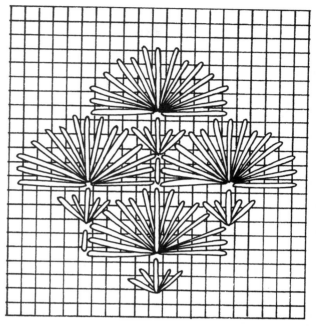

Feather. See Spanish Knot

Fern

Fern Stitch is worked, as shown in the diagram, by bringing the needle up at point A and taking an oblique stitch down to the right over four horizontal and three vertical threads of the canvas to point B. The needle is then brought up two vertical threads immediately to the left at point C, and another oblique stitch is taken up to the right over four horizontal and three vertical threads to point D. To commence a second similar stitch the needle is brought up four vertical threads of the canvas to the left and two horizontal threads down, at a point two horizontal threads below point A, where the first stitch started. The process is then continued by working in rows vertically from top to bottom of the area of canvas to be covered.

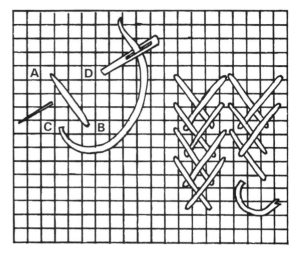

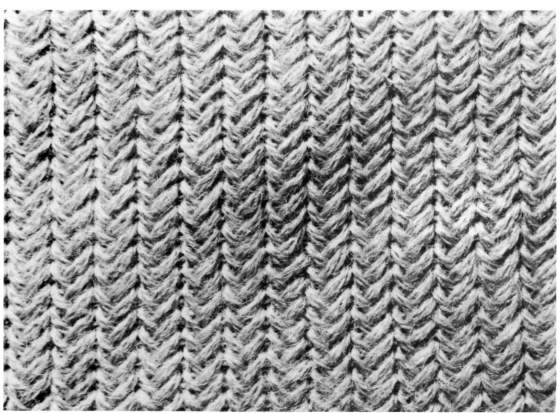

Figure. See Roumanian Couching

Fishbone

This stitch is usually worked diagonally over four intersections of the canvas and is tied down by a small diagonal stitch over the last intersection. A vertical row of these stitches is worked by beginning each stitch two horizontal threads of the canvas below the previous one. In the second row the stitches slope in the opposite direction, and each one is similarly tied down over the last intersection. Subsequent rows are worked in the same way and form a chevron type of pattern.

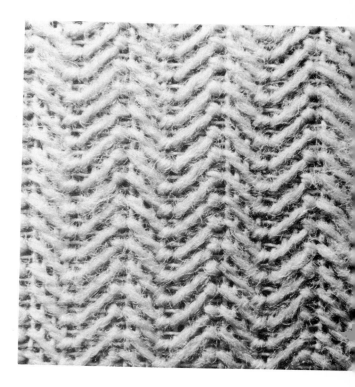

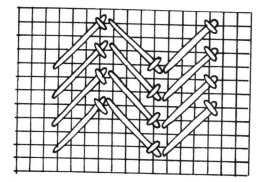

Fishbone — Horizontal

Fishbone Stitch can also be worked with the stitches all placed horizontally, instead of diagonally, as shown in the photograph and diagram.

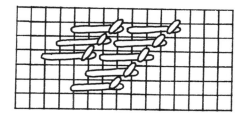

Fishbone — Stepped

In this version of Fishbone Stitch some groups of stitches are worked vertically and some horizontally. The groups, or rows, of stitches are, however, so placed that they follow a diagonal of the canvas. Working downwards from the top of the area to be covered, each of the horizontal stitches is placed not only one horizontal thread of the canvas below the stitch before it, but also one vertical thread further to the left, and each vertical stitch is not only one vertical thread to the left, but also one horizontal thread below the previous stitch. It is this which produces the stepped effect in the finished work. Each individual stitch is worked over four threads of the canvas, and the small stitch, which ties each stitch down, is worked over two threads.

Stepped Fishbone Stitch has a very firm appearance, with good coverage of the canvas.

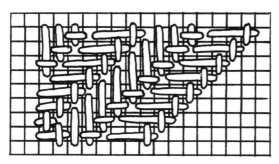

Flat or Satin Square

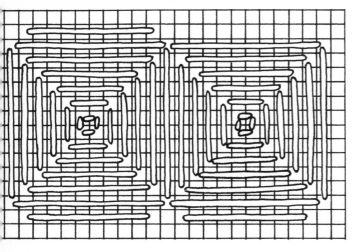

This stitch is made up of rows of diamond shapes, which are constructed by working groups of eleven straight stitches either vertically or horizontally. In the first row vertical straight stitches are worked over one, three, five, seven, nine, eleven, nine, seven, five, three and one horizontal threads of the canvas respectively, and one intersection of the canvas is left unworked between the diamond shapes. In the next row the groups of stitches are worked in the same order, but this time using eleven horizontal stitches to form the diamonds, which are fitted exactly into the spaces between the similar shapes in the first row.

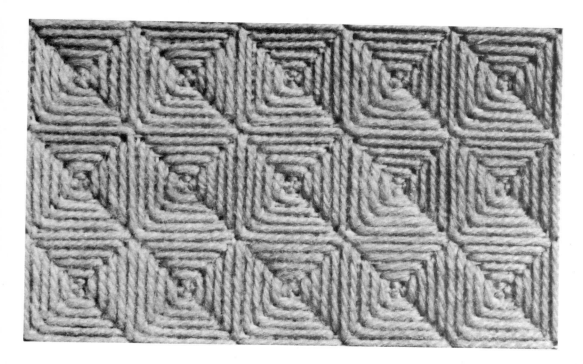

Floral

A cross stitch over two intersections of the canvas is worked first, followed by a group of three horizontal stitches over three vertical threads of the canvas. This is repeated to the end of the row, working horizontally. The second row starts with three vertical stitches over three horizontal threads of the canvas, which are worked immediately below the first cross stitch. This is followed by a cross stitch over three intersections of the canvas, and this process is continued to the end of the row. From this point on successive rows of stitches alternate in the same way as the first and second rows.

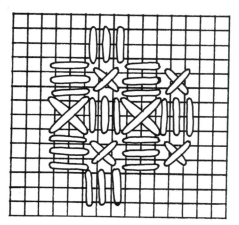

Florentine

One of the most popular stitches with beginners is also one which has been in constant use over a very long period. It is called Florentine or Flame Stitch, and in recent years it has also been known as Bargello Work. In its simplest form it consists of a series of vertical straight stitches, worked over four horizontal threads of the canvas, each stitch rising or falling by two threads above or below the last stitch. There are numerous variations of Florentine, but the best known and most popular way of working produces a zig-zag or flame pattern, which is accentuated by a skilful use of colour.

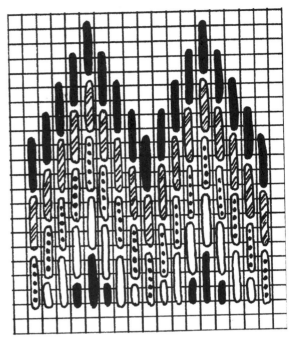

Florentine — Variation (Old Parisian)

In this variation of Florentine Stitch, which is
sometimes called Old Parisian or Double Parisian
Stitch, two vertical straight stitches, worked side
by side over three horizontal threads of the
canvas, alternate with two vertical stitches over
nine horizontal threads. The longer stitches
begin three horizontal threads above and end three
threads below the smaller stitches, thus leaving a
space between the groups of two longer stitches
in a row, into which the stitches of the second
row can be fitted. (See diagram)

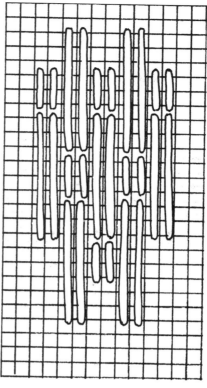

Flower

This stitch should be commenced at a point three vertical threads of the canvas in from the left-hand corner of the area to be covered and one horizontal thread down. A vertical stitch should then be worked from this point downwards over two horizontal threads of the canvas. One vertical thread further to the right another vertical stitch should be worked over four horizontal threads of the canvas, beginning one horizontal thread below the bottom end of the first stitch and ending one horizontal thread above the top of it. Another similar stitch is put in beside this second stitch, and a fourth vertical stitch is worked over two horizontal threads, similar to the first stitch and balancing it on the right-hand side. Two vertical threads of the canvas are now left uncovered, before a second similar group of stitches is worked and the process is repeated until a full row of such stitches has been worked. When working the row immediately below, similar groups of four straight stitches are used, but this time they are worked

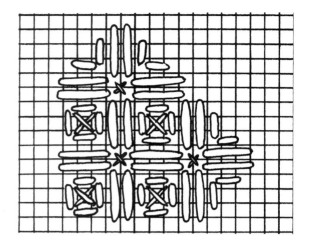

horizontally and are fitted between the groups in the row before. A tiny cross stitch over one intersection of the canvas is worked between these groups of horizontal straight stitches, and a cross stitch over two intersections is put in between the groups of vertical stitches.

Four Part Eye

This stitch, which is best worked diagonally across the canvas, gives a fine, very closely woven appearance, if it is worked over two threads on a 16 mesh canvas. It should be started with the working of an eye stitch, consisting of two vertical and two horizontal stitches over two threads of the canvas, all going down into the centre hole. Small back stitches are then worked over the single intersections of the canvas left between individual stitches in the eye stitches. The diagram shows the stitch worked over two threads of the canvas, and it also gives a larger version, worked over four threads, with the diagonal stitches taken over two intersections.

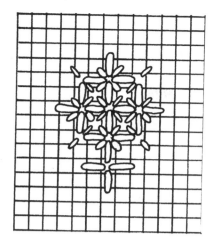

Four, Three, Two Cross

This is a square stitch, worked over four threads of the canvas. First of all three vertical stitches over four, three and two horizontal threads of the canvas respectively are worked side by side, the first stitch forming the left-hand side of the square and the other two having their top ends on the top edge of the square, with their lower ends each rising one horizontal thread above the lower end of the stitch before it. A group of three horizontal stitches of the same size is then put in at right-angles to the first group of stitches, so that a square of stitches is formed, and this is finished off when a diagonal stitch is taken from the bottom left-hand corner to the top right.

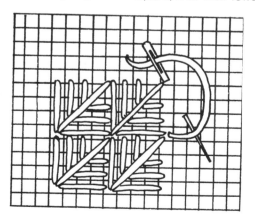

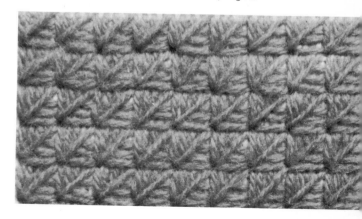

French

This stitch is generally worked diagonally across the canvas, but it can be worked horizontally to give the same effect.

A vertical stitch is first worked over four horizontal threads of the canvas, and the needle is brought out two threads down and one to the left of the first stitch. A small horizontal stitch is now taken to the right over one canvas thread and the first stitch. The needle is brought out in the same hole as the beginning of the first stitch, and a similar vertical stitch is put in beside the first one, the needle entering the same hole at the top. Finally, the needle is brought out two threads down and one to the right of the second vertical stitch and is inserted in the centre hole between the two stitches, thus tying the second one down.

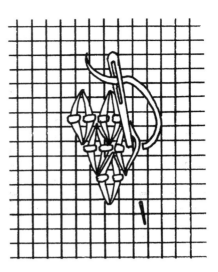

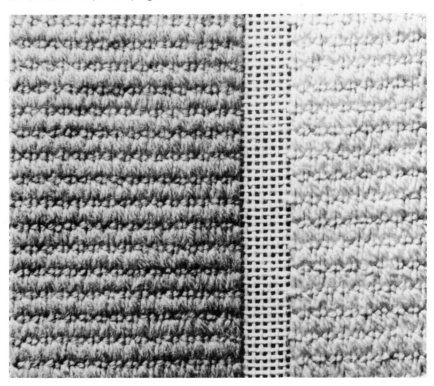

Worked in silk on 16-mesh canvas

Symphony of Light worked by May Wellard.
(Size: 109 cm x 81 cm – 43 in. x 31¾ in.)
The central area of this very attractive panel consists of a
circle of gold leather on to which topaz jewels have been
applied, and this is surrounded by an area of long Satin
stitches, worked in artificial raffia, around which another
circle of leather has been applied to the canvas. Most of the
remainder of the panel is worked in Tent Stitch and Gobelin
Stitch, with Mosaic Stitch for the background. The
colouring used in every part of this panel, including the
background, is very carefully shaded. Vegetable-dyed wools
have been used, together with raffia and Goldfingering, on
16 mesh, single thread canvas.

Sunrise at Sea designed by Mary Rhodes and worked by
Shirley Windle
(Size: approx. 114 cm x 58 cm – 45 in. x 23½ in.)
A partly worked panel, which was designed to show
movement of line. A wide variety of stitches has been used,
including Cashmere, Crossed-cornered Cushion, English,
Milanese, Portuguese Stem, Rhodes and Stem Stitch with
many others. 16 mesh single thread canvas

Worked in wool on 14-mesh canvas

French Knot

For this stitch the yarn should be brought up through the canvas at the exact spot where the knot is required and should be held firmly between the thumb and first finger of the left hand, whilst the needle is twisted once or twice around it. The twists of yarn should be tightened on the needle, the point of which should then be turned away from the worker and inserted over one intersection of the canvas. It could really be described as almost a knotted tent stitch.

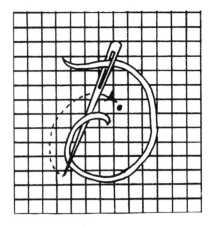

French — Variation (Sometimes known as Renaissance Tied)

This stitch, which covers four horizontal and six vertical threads of the canvas, is generally worked diagonally across the canvas, but it can be worked horizontally to give the same effect. A vertical stitch is first worked over four horizontal threads of the canvas, and it is tied down in the centre by the working of a back stitch over two vertical threads of the canvas. The yarn is then brought out from the same hole at the beginning of the first stitch, and another vertical stitch is taken down into the same hole at the base of the first stitch, and it is then tied down two vertical threads of the canvas to the right by means of another back stitch over two vertical threads. A third vertical stitch is put in, emerging from and going down into the same holes in the canvas as the other two vertical stitches, and this one is tied

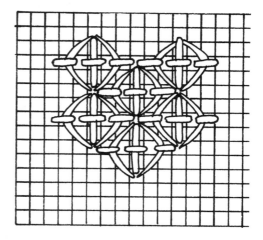

down by a similar back stitch over two vertical threads, which draws the vertical stitch two vertical threads to the left.

Gate

This new stitch can be worked in rows horizontally, vertically or diagonally across the canvas. It is formed by working four vertical straight stitches over six horizontal threads of the canvas. A stitch is then taken from the bottom of the outside stitch on the right to the top of the second stitch on the left, and another stitch goes from the bottom of the outside stitch on the left to the top of the second stitch in from the right. From this point the needle is finally brought up three vertical threads of the canvas to the left and two horizontal threads down, and a horizontal stitch, extending over five vertical threads of the canvas, is taken across the whole group of stitches worked so far. Proceeding horizontally across the area to be covered, the next group of stitches is worked with the first of the four vertical straight stitches beginning at a point five vertical threads of the canvas to the right of the last vertical stitch in the first group. This leaves three vertical threads of the canvas quite clear between two groups of stitches in the horizontal row, and into this space another Gate Stitch can be fitted. It commences, however, three horizontal threads of the canvas down — a half-drop — and is worked in an inverted

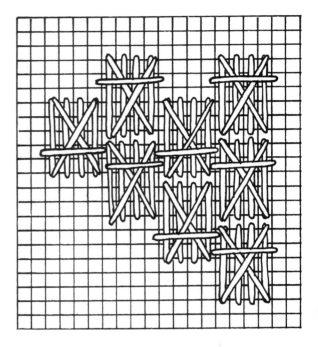

form, so that the horizontal bar is placed across the lower half of the main block of stitches and not at the top. (See the diagram.)

Ghiordes Knot (Turkey Rug Knot)

This stitch is started from the front of the canvas and is worked from the bottom left-hand corner of the area to be covered. The loose end of the yarn is held between fore-finger and thumb of the left hand, whilst the needle is taken under one vertical thread of the canvas, moving from right to left. Then, with the working yarn held loosely, the needle should be put under the next vertical thread of the canvas to the right and, moving once more from right to left, it should be brought up through the same hole in the canvas where the first stitch was started, and in such a way that it passes under the loop of the working yarn. This loop should then be tightened by pulling the two ends of the yarn down firmly. The process is repeated under the next vertical thread of the canvas to the right, whilst a loop of the yarn is at the same time held down by the thumb, and it is continued thus, until a whole row of stitches has been completed. The working yarn should be cut at the end of the row, and the next row should

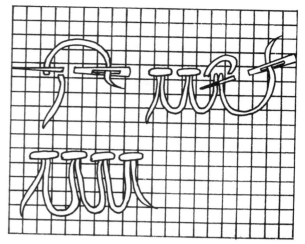

be begun on the left, two threads of the canvas above and one thread to the right of the first stitch in the first row, so that the rows of stitches will be staggered. Finally, the loops can be cut and trimmed to form a pile (approximate depth 6mm — ¼ in.).

Gobelin

The name Gobelin covers a whole group of straight satin stitches.

To work the basic form of this stitch, one should proceed in horizontal rows from top to bottom of the area to be covered, the first row being worked from right to left, the second from left to right, and so on. Start by taking a diagonal stitch upwards over two horizontal threads of the canvas and one vertical thread to the right. The next stitch is then begun two horizontal threads of the canvas down from this point and two vertical threads to the left and is worked in the same way as the first stitch. This process is repeated until a complete row of stitches has been worked across the canvas. The second row begins with the needle being brought up through the canvas at the point where the next to last stitch in the first row had begun and then being taken down over two horizontal threads of the canvas and one vertical thread to the left. For the next stitch in the row the needle is brought up two horizontal threads above this point and two vertical threads to the right, and the process is repeated until the second row has been worked.

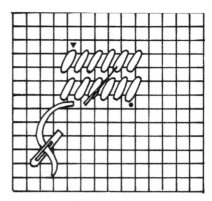

Gobelin Stitch also known as Gros Point

It is advisable always to work the stitch in this way, in order to get the maximum amount of wool on the reverse side of the canvas, and thus give the finished embroidery a fuller and better appearance. The photograph shows the stitch worked on double thread canvas.

Gobelin — Crossed

A row of vertical straight stitches is worked, each one over six horizontal threads of the canvas and each one tied down at its centre point by a cross stitch over two horizontal and two vertical threads. Between the straight stitches in a row, spaces of the width of two vertical threads of the canvas are left empty, and into these spaces the vertical stitches forming the next row are fitted, each individual straight stitch being dropped four horizontal threads below the row above, so that the second row encroaches on the first by two horizontal threads.

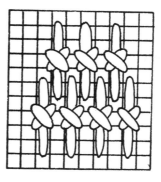

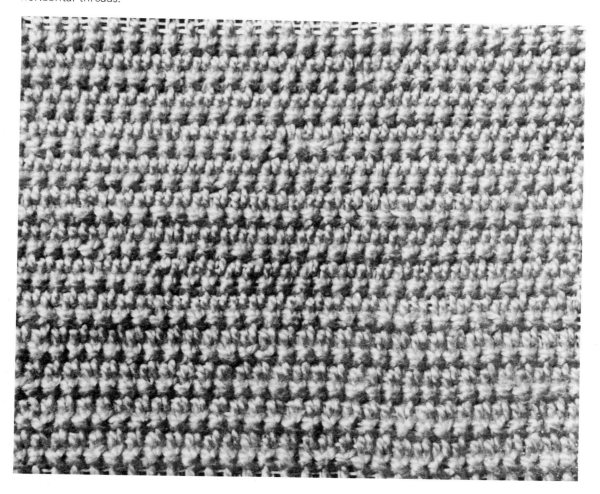

Gobelin — Encroaching

In the many variations of Encroaching Gobelin Stitch rows of the stitch are so worked that individual stitches encroach into the spaces between stitches in adjacent rows. This method of working may be used with vertical or diagonal versions of this stitch, and the individual elements of each stitch may be single or double.

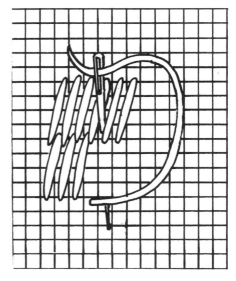

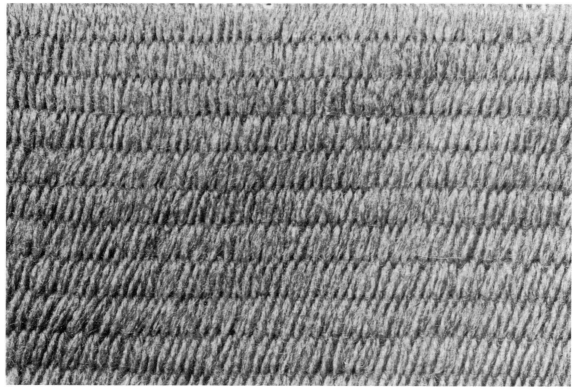

Gobelin Filling

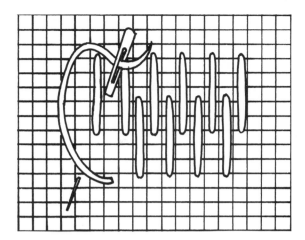

Gobelin Variation

Gobelin — Oblique (Also known as Oblique Slav)

In this version of Gobelin Stitch the individual stitches are taken up over three horizontal threads of the canvas and over one vertical thread to the right.

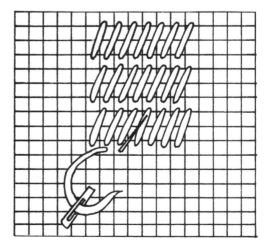

Gobelin — Plaited

To begin this stitch the needle is brought up through the canvas at a point four horizontal threads of the canvas below the top left-hand corner of the area to be covered. A stitch is taken upwards from left to right over two vertical and four horizontal threads. The needle is then brought out four horizontal threads immediately below, and the second stitch is put in, leaving two threads of the canvas empty between it and the first stitch. This process is repeated to the end of the row. The second row starts with a stitch worked two horizontal threads directly below the first stitch in the previous row. Working upwards from right to left over two vertical and four horizontal threads this stitch encroaches by two horizontal threads over the stitch above it.

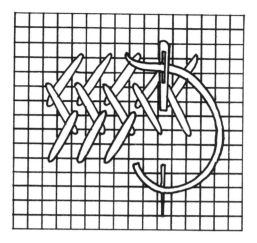

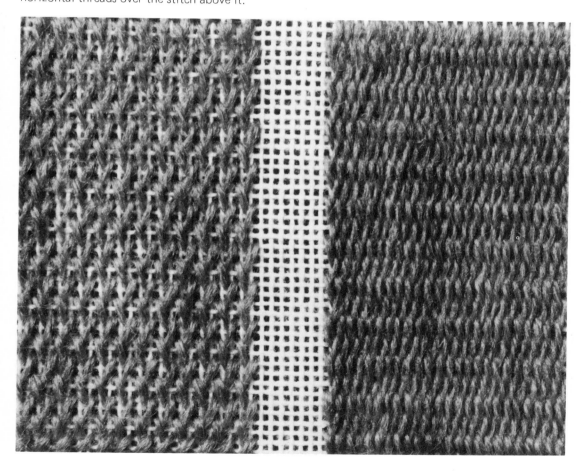

Gobelin — Straight

This consists simply of rows of vertical straight stitches, worked into every hole in the canvas over two or more horizontal threads.

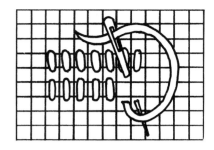

Gobelin — Tied

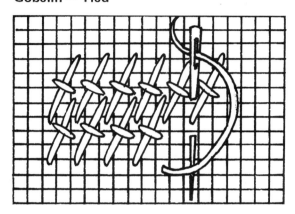

In this variation of Gobelin Stitch the individual oblique stitches are worked over five horizontal and two vertical threads of the canvas, and they are placed so that there is a space of two threads of the canvas between them. Each stitch is tied down at the centre by means of a small oblique stitch over two vertical and one horizontal thread of the canvas. The second row of stitches fits into the spaces between the stitches in the first row and each stitch encroaches over the corresponding stitch in the previous row by two horizontal threads of the canvas.

Gordian Knot. See Braid

Greek. See Long-Legged Cross

Gros Point

Certain canvas-work stitches are sometimes referred to by this name. The term has been used to describe stitches worked over two or more horizontal threads of the canvas and has been applied to such stitches as Gobelin Stitch, Cross Stitch and Florentine Stitch, with their variations.

Guilloche

Groups of three vertical stitches over four horizontal threads of the canvas alternate with groups of three horizontal stitches over two vertical threads.

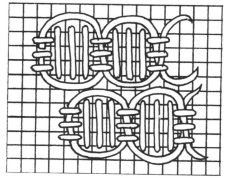

A length of yarn, either of the same or of a contrasting colour, is then threaded up through the first group of horizontal stitches, is taken over and around the top of the first group of three vertical stitches and down and around the lower edge of the next group of three vertical stitches, passing through the loop of the three horizontal stitches on the way. This process is continued to the end of the row, and on the return journey from right to left the yarn completes the encirclement of the groups of stitches. In the second row, as the diagram shows, the groups of three vertical stitches are placed under the groups of horizontal stitches in the row above, and vice versa.

The photograph shows Guilloche Stitch also being used as an expanding stitch.

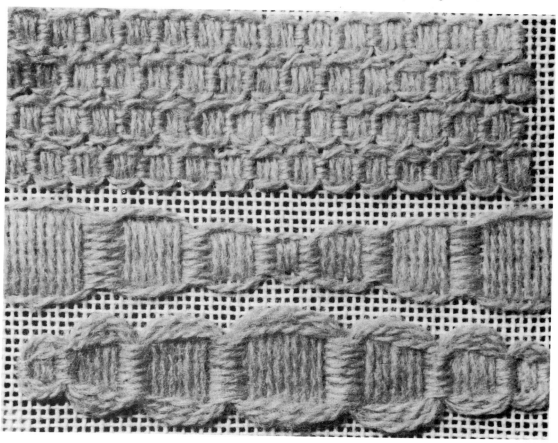

Half-drop-tied

Two vertical straight stitches, worked side by side over six horizontal threads of the canvas, are tied in the centre by a horizontal stitch over three vertical canvas threads. These groups of stitches are worked in rows horizontally, with three vertical threads of the canvas left unworked between the groups, in order to accommodate the groups of stitches in the following row, which encroaches by three horizontal threads over the previous row.

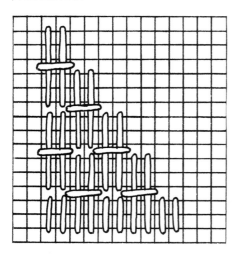

Half Eye

Half of an Eye Stitch is worked over eight horizontal and four vertical threads of the canvas, and the groups of stitches so formed are placed so that they make a half-drop pattern across the area to be covered. Eye Stitches should always be worked with the needle coming up on the outside edge and going down into the centre hole. It is advisable to use a yarn which can be pulled quite tightly in order to open up the hole, or a stiletto can be used for the purpose.

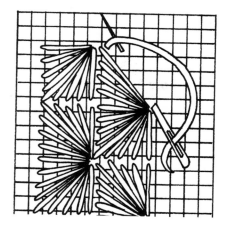

Half Rhodes. See Rhodes Half Half-drop

Half Rhodes — Plaited. See Rhodes Half-Plaited

Herringbone

Herringbone Stitch was in the past always considered to be a linear stitch, but in recent times it has been pressed into service as a filling stitch, and this fact seems to account for the slight difficulty which can be experienced in working the return rows correctly.

The stitch is worked over four intersections of the canvas. The needle is brought up at the bottom left-hand corner of the first stitch, and the yarn is taken up over four intersections of the canvas to the right. Then the needle is brought up again two vertical threads of the canvas to the left, and a second stitch over four intersections is taken down to the right, passing over the first stitch. The needle is again brought up two vertical threads to the left, and the process is repeated and continued to the end of the row.

When this stitch is used to fill an area of the canvas, all the rows of stitches can be worked from left to right, as described above, each one being fastened off at the right-hand end, before the next row is started on the left. In doing this each row is placed two horizontal threads of the canvas below the row above, so that the individual stitches fit exactly together. If, however, it is decided to work one row from left to right and the next row from right to left, the first stitch of the second row should begin two horizontal threads of the canvas immediately below the top right-hand end of the last stitch in the row above, and the yarn should be taken down over four intersections of the canvas to the left. The needle is then brought up six vertical threads to the right, and the yarn is taken up over four intersections of the canvas, passing over the first stitch on the way. The needle is again brought out two vertical threads to the left, and the process is repeated to the end of the row. Care must be taken, however, when working these reverse rows, to pass the yarn each time under the first stitch in the previous group, as shown in the diagram.

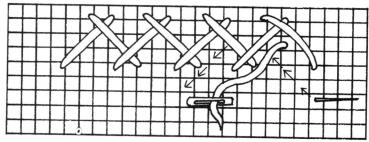

Showing the start of the second row

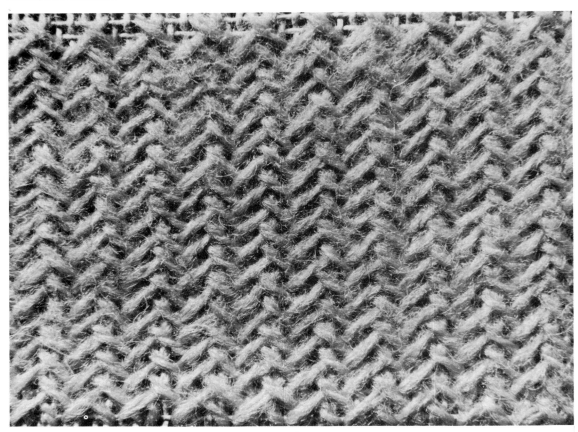

Herringbone — Double (Also known as Indian)

In doing this stitch two rows of Herringbone Stitch are worked one above the other, so that they interlace, and the yarn used in forming the stitches passes over and under itself in a regular sequence. To accomplish this the stitches must be large enough to allow room for the two rows to fit neatly into one another. In the diagram each individual stitch is taken over six intersections of the canvas. There is a difference from the normal in working the stitch at the top, where the individual stitch, which goes diagonally from top left to bottom right, is taken under the stitch before it and not over it, as in normal Herringbone Stitch.

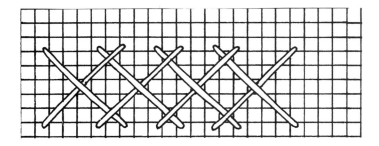

Herringbone — Double — Interlaced (Also known as German)

This attractive stitch is worked on a basis of Double Herringbone Stitch, which must have been absolutely correctly constructed itself, so that the interlacing thread can follow the path as shown in the diagram with the correct sequence of 'overs' and 'unders'. The foundation stitch should be worked quite loosely, in order to accommodate the lacing yarn easily and avoid any pulling together of the foundation stitch.

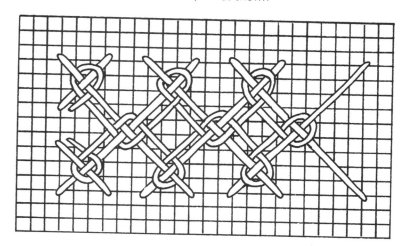

Double Interlaced with Tent

Herringbone — Double Interlaced Filling

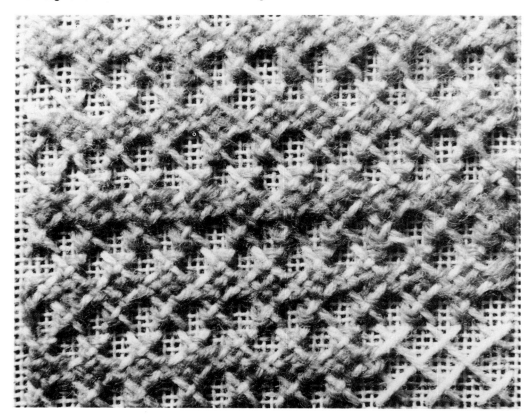

Herringbone — Interlaced

The interlacing of this stitch can only be carried out correctly, if the version of Herringbone Stitch, on which it is based, is worked with the needle being slipped **under** the previous stitch each time and not **over** it, as is the usual way of working. When the foundation has been worked, a second yarn is used to lace around the stitches where they cross. This yarn makes two complete circles around each upper cross and one-and-a-half circles around each lower cross, and it interlaces over and under the foundation stitch, as well as over and under itself. See the diagram.

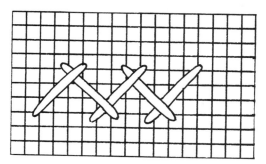

Herringbone used for Interlaced Stitch

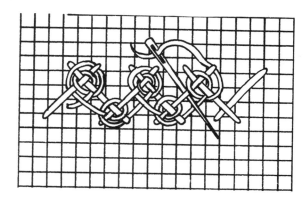

Herringbone Squared or Multiplait

This stitch starts with a cross stitch, worked over an even number of threads of the canvas. The diagram shows the cross stitch worked over two vertical and two horizontal threads of the canvas. A series of Herringbone Stitches is then worked around it and around one another to fill the shape required, beginning when the needle is brought up one thread to the left of the bottom left-hand arm of the cross and is taken up to the right over three intersections of the canvas to a point one horizontal thread above the top right-hand arm of the cross. The needle is then brought out two vertical threads to the left, and the yarn is taken down over three intersections of the canvas to the right to a point one vertical thread to the right of the bottom right-hand arm of the cross. Again the needle is brought up two horizontal threads above, and the yarn is taken over three intersections of the canvas down to the left to a point one horizontal thread of the canvas below the bottom left-hand arm of the cross. Now the needle is brought up again two vertical threads to the right, and another stitch is put in over three intersections of the canvas up to the left to a point one vertical thread to the left of the top left-hand arm of the cross. The cross stitch is now enclosed by Herringbone Stitches, which are then

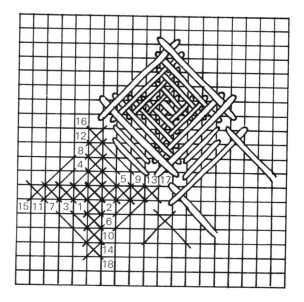

continued around one another as shown by the numbers on the diagram and can be extended further to cover any size required.

Herringbone — Variation

This is the same as Herringbone Stitch, in working from left to right, but, in working the reverse rows from right to left, there is a difference, which causes a reverse of the overlap of the individual stitches. To work these reverse rows from right to left, the needle is brought out two horizontal threads of the canvas immediately below the bottom right-hand corner of the last stitch in the row above. The yarn is then taken up over four intersections of the canvas to the left, and the needle is brought out again two vertical threads back to the right, and a stitch is put in down over four intersections to the left. The needle is again brought out two vertical threads to the right, and the process is repeated until the row is complete.

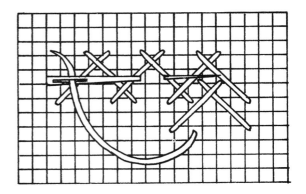

Hound's Tooth

This square stitch can be worked over any number of threads of the canvas, provided that the yarn used is matched to the size of the stitch. The photograph shows the stitch worked over four horizontal and four vertical threads of the canvas. The work begins with a diagonal stitch from bottom left to top right over four intersections of the canvas. The needle is then brought up at the bottom right-hand corner of the square, and the yarn is looped over the diagonal stitch and taken back down again through the same hole in the canvas. Then from the top left-hand corner a second loop is made to go through the first loop

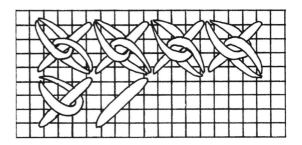

and under the diagonal stitch, before it also is taken back down into the hole in the canvas from which it emerged.

Hour-glass

This stitch can be worked either horizontally or diagonally across the canvas. It forms a half-drop pattern, which is based upon an Oblong Cross Stitch, worked over six horizontal and two vertical threads of the canvas, with a horizontal straight stitch, worked over two vertical threads, placed across the top of the cross.

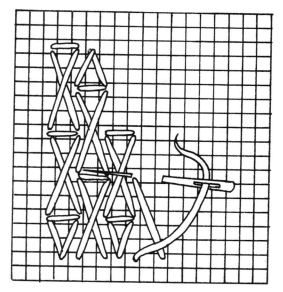

Worked either horizontally or diagonally

Hungarian

This is an attractive stitch, which is useful for shading a large area, as it can be worked either in one colour or in rows of contrasting colours. It consists of three vertical stitches, worked over two, four and two horizontal threads of the canvas respectively. Two vertical threads of the canvas, or one hole, are left uncovered between the groups of three stitches in a row, so that the long stitches of the following row can be worked into the space, and the rows are thus interlocked.

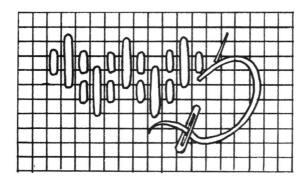

Hungarian — Variation

Hungarian Grounding

This heading covers a wide range of stitch-patterns, built up by working vertical straight stitches over a predetermined number of horizontal threads of the canvas, as is shown in the diagram. Originally this type of pattern was always worked in several shades of one colour, but today it is often worked in shades of a number of different colours. It is also today often mistakenly called Florentine Stitch, and quite recently, and just as mistakenly, it has been known as Bargello.

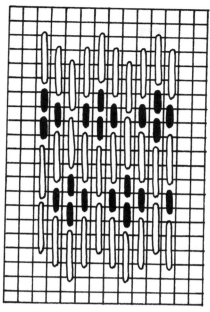

Hungarian Grounding — Variation

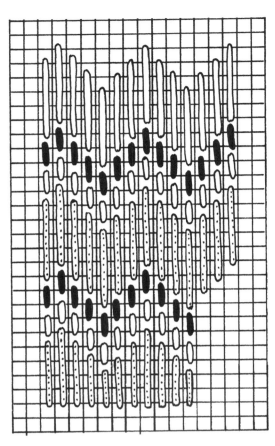

Hurdle

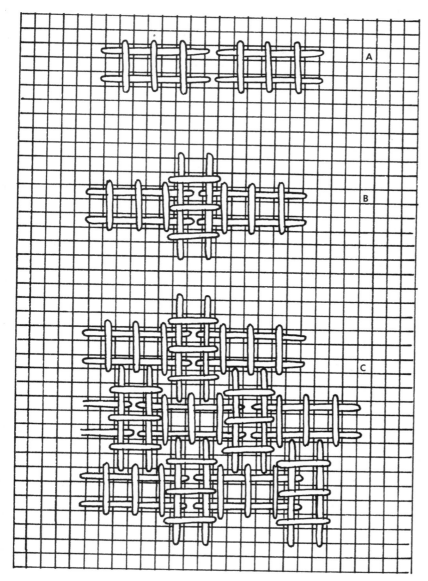

To work this stitch from left to right across the canvas, one should start from a point three horizontal threads down from the top left-hand corner of the area to be covered. Groups of two horizontal straight stitches, each one over eight vertical threads of the canvas, are then worked side by side across the canvas, the two stitches being placed so that one is immediately below the other, with a space of two horizontal threads of the canvas between them. Each group of two horizontal stitches is then worked over with three vertical straight stitches, each one being over four horizontal threads of the canvas and so placed

that there is a space of two vertical threads between them. The next stage in the process is to work other groups of stitches similar to those just described, but in a vertical position instead of horizontally, and to place one such group to straddle each of the points where the original groups of long horizontal stitches meet one another. A second row of these Hurdle Stitches is worked by moving the groups of stitches in the second row along to the right by half of one Hurdle Stitch, at the same time leaving one horizontal thread of the canvas clear between the rows.

Indian. See Herringbone — Double

Interlaced Cross

This is a square stitch, which is generally worked over four threads of the canvas and is made up of six diagonal stitches. It can, however, be worked over six or eight threads, but in that case a somewhat thicker yarn is needed. The basic Cross Stitch starts with a diagonal stitch, taken from the bottom right-hand corner of the square to the top left-hand corner, and is then crossed by another diagonal stitch from the bottom left-hand corner to the top right-hand corner of the square. The third stitch starts one vertical thread of the canvas to the right of the bottom left-hand corner of the square and goes up to the right to a point one horizontal thread below the top right-hand corner. The fourth stitch starts one vertical thread to the left of the bottom right-hand corner of the square and goes up to the left to a point one horizontal thread below the top left-hand corner of the square. The fifth stitch starts one horizontal thread above the bottom left-hand corner and

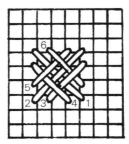

goes up to the right to a point one vertical thread to the left of the top right-hand corner of the square. The final stitch starts one vertical thread to the right of the top left-hand corner of the square and goes down to the right to a point one horizontal thread above the bottom right-hand corner. In making this last stitch the yarn is taken over two of the previous stitches, but is slipped under the third one, before being taken down through the canvas.

Interlacing. See Maltese Cross

Interlocking Leaf

This charming stitch was evolved by working a row of Leaf Stitches and then reversing it to form the second row. The eventual shape of individual leaves is, however, different from that of the original Leaf Stitch, and the working can either be done in separate rows across the canvas, with the second row reversed and fitting into the first row, or with the two rows worked together as one unit. If the working is to follow a curved shape, it is better to work the top row only first, and then fit the reversed section into it, so that any necessary adjustments can be made more easily.

The working should be started with a vertical straight stitch, taken down over six horizontal threads of the canvas. Then two other stitches, each over five threads, are put in on either side of the first stitch, one starting at a point one thread down and one to the right, and the other one thread down and one to the left of the point where the first stitch began, and all these stitches

finishing by going down into the same hole in the canvas. A stitch is then put in on either side of these three, one starting at a point one thread down and one to the left, and the other one thread down and one to the right of the outer stitches in the group of three, with both stitches finishing in the same hole in the canvas, which is one thread immediately below the bottom point of the initial group of three stitches. Other similar pairs of stitches should now be put in, each pair beginning and ending one thread below the stitches above them. If only the top row of Leaf Stitches is being worked first, then only two extra pairs of these stitches will now have to be added, but, if the whole unit is being worked, it will need five more pairs, followed by another of the groups of three stitches going down into one hole in the canvas, but this time worked in reverse and made to fit into the area of stitches just worked, either on its right side or on its left. See the diagram and the photograph of the worked stitch.

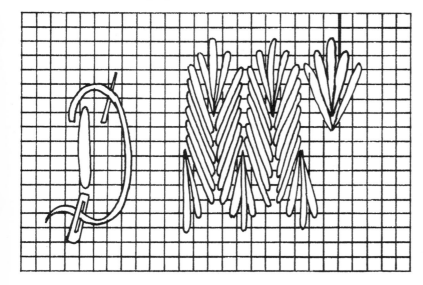

Islamic

This is a square stitch, worked over eight threads of the canvas, which gives a very attractive square tile effect. The working begins with a stitch from the top left-hand corner of the square down into the centre hole. Two other stitches, one from a point two vertical threads of the canvas to the right of this corner of the square, and another from a point two horizontal threads down from the corner, are also taken down into the centre hole. Three similar stitches are put in from each other corner of the square, and a large upright cross over six threads of the canvas, starting with the vertical stitch, is then worked over the centre hole. Other square groups of stitches are worked, starting from the same corner holes, and an upright cross over four threads of the canvas is worked over the spot where four complete groups meet. Finally, a straight stitch over four threads is worked between the corner upright crosses.

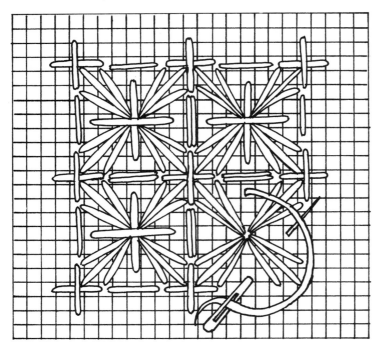

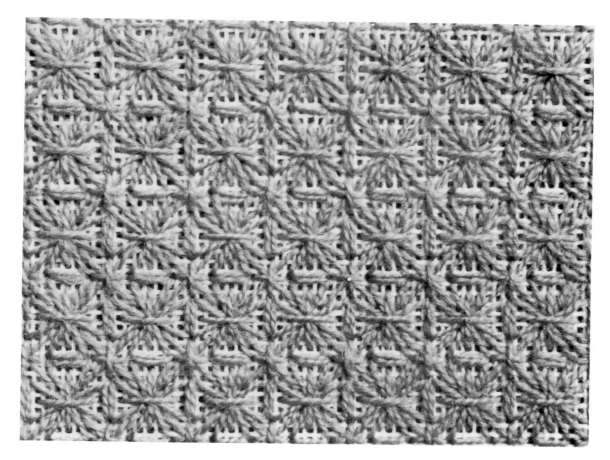

Islamic — Variation (Also known as Leviathan Stitch)

Although there is only a slight difference between the working of Islamic Stitch and of this Variation, the finished effect is quite different, the main stress in the Variation being upon the diagonals, rather than upon the outline of the square. The three stitches from each corner of the square are closer together, as there is only one thread of the canvas between them here, rather than two. There are two extra stitches in each quarter of the square, one on each side of the groups of three stitches. These extra stitches start from points which are three threads of the canvas in from the corners of the square and one thread from the sides towards the centre, and they all go down into the hole in the centre of the square. The central upright cross in the Variation is over four threads of the canvas, instead of six, and the upright crosses at the corners of the squares in the Islamic Stitch are moved up to the centres of the sides of the squares in the Variation.

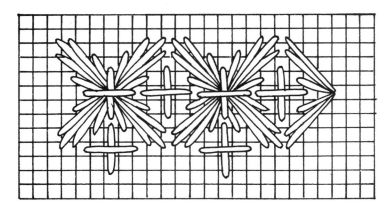

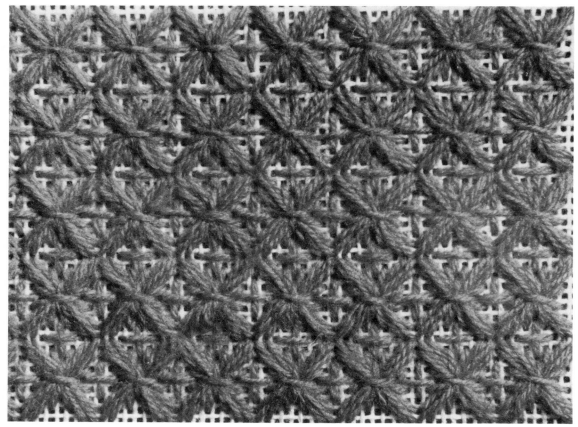

Italian Two-sided

This stitch consists of four individual stitches, three of which radiate from the bottom left-hand corner of a square, which extends over four threads of the canvas, and one stitch, which is taken from the bottom right-hand corner of the square to the top left-hand corner, thus passing over the other diagonal and forming a cross within a square of straight stitches, when all the other adjoining stitches have been worked. The yarn is brought out at the bottom right-hand corner of the square, when one group of four stitches has been completed, ready to begin the next group.

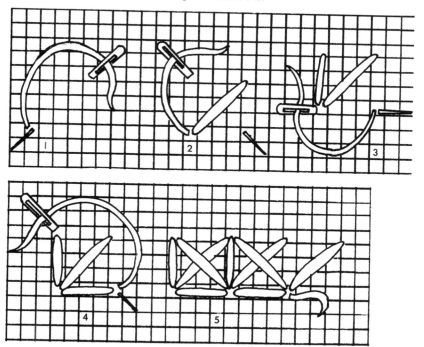

Jacquard

This stitch is very useful for working over large areas. It is worked in stepped rows. A row of stitches, worked over two intersections of the canvas, is put in, with the number of stitches in a 'step' being determined by the worker. This number, once decided upon, must remain constant throughout the whole of the working. The 'steps' of larger stitches are followed by the same number of tent stitches, which are, in turn, followed by more of the larger stitches, and so on.

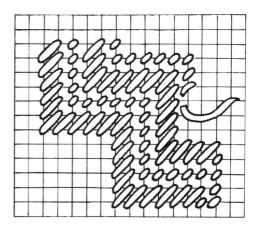

Knitted 1

This stitch is formed by working vertical rows of oblique stitches, each stitch over two intersections of the canvas. The direction of the individual stitches alternates, with the stitches in one row inclined downwards from left to right, and those in the next row from right to left.

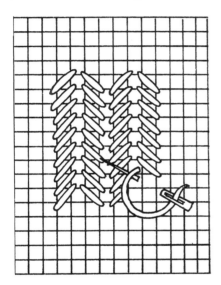

Knitted 2 (Known as Stocking Stitch on double canvas)

This stitch is worked in vertical rows downwards, and the working produces a chain effect. Individual stitches are worked over one vertical and four horizontal threads of the canvas, and the second and subsequent stitches start two horizontal threads below the previous stitch. In the second row the stitches start two vertical threads of the canvas to the right of the corresponding stitch in the first row, and the yarn goes down into the same hole in the canvas.

If necessary, this stitch can be worked over any even number of horizontal threads of the canvas.

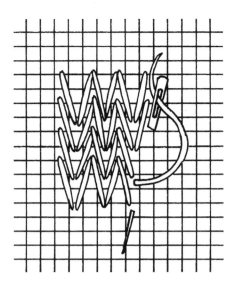

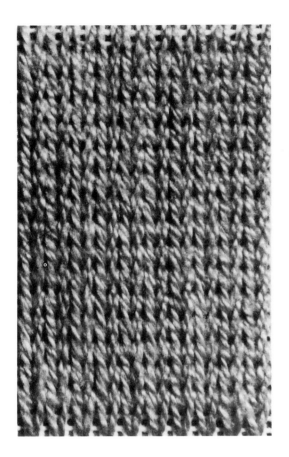

The diagram below shows the stitch worked on double canvas.

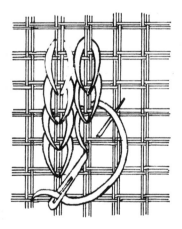

Knitting

This stitch is based on an elongated cross stitch, worked over four horizontal and two vertical threads of the canvas. It is worked in vertical rows downwards, with the second stitch beginning two horizontal threads below where the first stitch started and overlapping it. This latter fact causes a plaited effect to be given to the work. All the top stitches in each cross must be in the same direction.

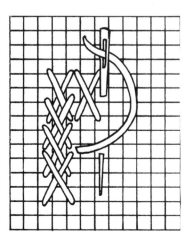

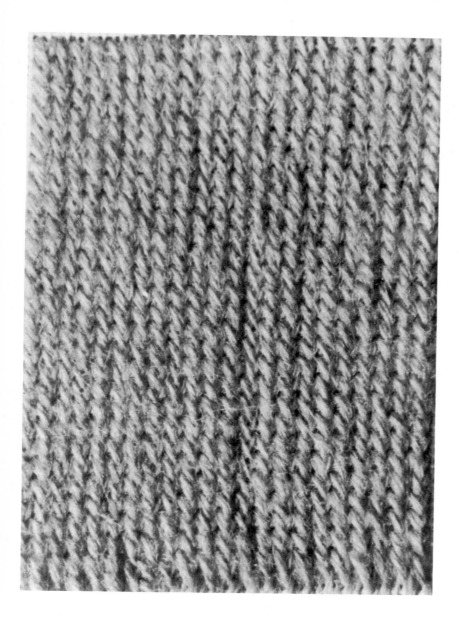

Knot. See Bullion

Knotted Tufting

This stitch is worked with the yarn on the front of the canvas, and the work is started from the bottom of the area to be covered. The needle is first taken down through the canvas, leaving a short length of the yarn on the surface, and it is brought up at a point one horizontal thread up and two vertical threads to the left. The needle is again taken down three vertical threads directly to the right and is brought up again at a point one horizontal thread down and two vertical threads back to the left. The yarn is now pulled firm before commencing the second stitch, which is started four vertical threads of the canvas to the right, leaving a loop of yarn on the surface. At least two horizontal threads of the canvas should be left between rows of this stitch. Finally, when

a sufficient area has been covered, the loops of yarn left on the surface are cut to the length required.

This stitch can be worked over two vertical threads of the canvas instead of three, in which case the ends of the yarn forming the loops should be brought out of the same hole, with no canvas thread between them.

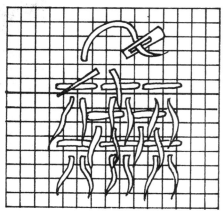

Knotted Zigzag

This can be a very useful stitch for working a border. The photograph shows it worked with a fine, three-ply wool on 16 mesh canvas over three vertical and three horizontal threads, but, with a thicker yarn on coarser canvas, it would work very successfully as a textured stitch, particularly for working trees and landscapes. The working of the left-hand stitch is shown at A in the diagram, where the yarn is taken over the top of the needle from right to left and is then brought back under it, and the working of the right-hand stitch is shown at B in the diagram, with the yarn being taken from left to right over and under the tip of the needle.

This stitch is, in fact, a version of Coral Knot Stitch and is the result of working the stitch in a zigzag.

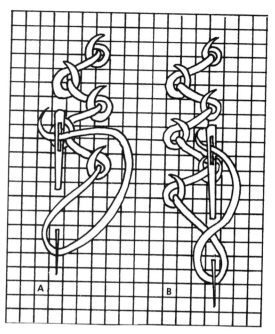

Laid Oriental. See Roumanian Couching

Lattice

This stitch is based on a square over eight threads
of the canvas. Starting in the middle of each side
of the square with two threads of the canvas
between them, two stitches are taken over four
threads down into the centre hole. The ends of
the stitches are sealed with a back stitch at the
point where they meet the edge of the square.
These groups of stitches are worked in rows
horizontally from left to right across the area to
be covered, the groups in subsequent rows being
fitted into the spaces between those in previous
rows. Finally, an oblong cross stitch over three
horizontal and two vertical threads of the canvas
is worked in the spaces between the original
groups of stitches, as shown in the diagram.

This stitch is more effective if it is worked in
two colours.

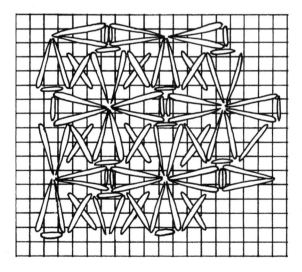

Lattice Band — Twisted

This attractive border stitch is worked on a foundation of Double Herringbone Stitch. The interlacing is worked in two rows, the upper row being worked first from left to right, and the lower row next from right to left. The yarn for the interlacing is brought up through the canvas at the beginning of each row and is taken down again at the end, all the interlacing being worked on the surface, as is shown in the diagram.

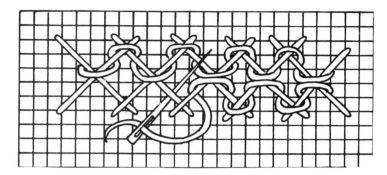

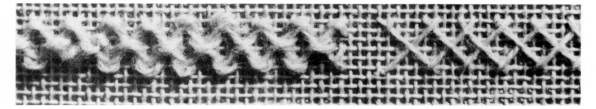

Lattice Square — Twisted

This stitch is worked in a similar manner to Lattice Band. The foundation lines are worked first and consist of long single oblique stitches, all worked in one direction, with another set of similar stitches worked at right-angles and forming a trellis by being interlaced over and under the first set of stitches. On this foundation another yarn, which can be of the same or of a contrasting colour, is then interlaced in rows from left to right and back from right to left, in the same way as in the working of Lattice Band and as shown in the diagram.

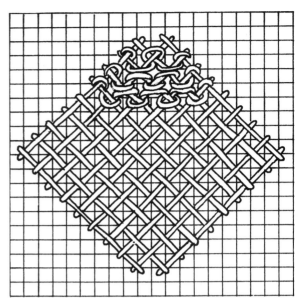

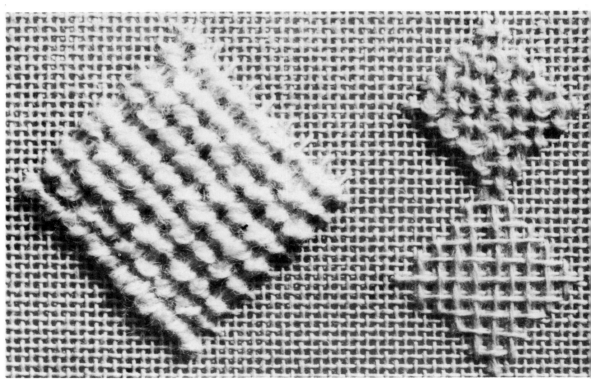

Leaf 1

This stitch begins with the working of a straight stitch down over six horizontal threads of the canvas. Then two stitches are put in, each one over five threads, one starting one thread down and one thread to the right, and the other starting one thread down and one thread to the left of the point where the first stitch started, and both stitches finishing in the hole where the first stitch ended. The next stitch starts another one thread of the canvas down and one thread further to the left and is taken down into the hole in the canvas immediately beneath the previous stitch.

This is followed by three stitches of equal length, the first of which starts one thread lower and one thread further to the left than the stitch before it, with the other two stitches placed one thread lower each time, but directly beneath each other. The other side of the Leaf Stitch is completed in the same way. The final stitch down the centre of the leaf, as shown in the diagram, is optional. The leaf shape can be made wider or narrower by varying the number of threads of the canvas covered by each single stitch. The diagram also shows this stitch worked diagonally as a variation and in the form of a star.

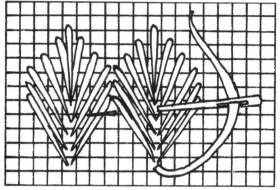

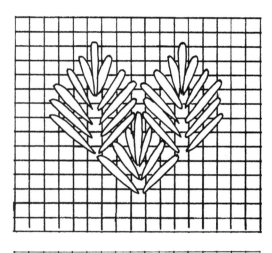

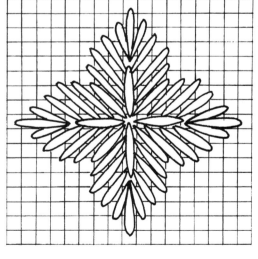

Leaf 1 continued

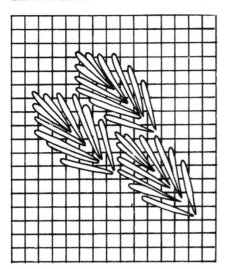

Leaf 2

This stitch begins with a diagonal stitch over two intersections of the canvas, going down from left to right and having a stitch, which is placed one thread on either side of it, going down into the same hole in the canvas. Two more stitches are worked on either side of this group of three, each separated from the next by one thread of the canvas, and all four going down into the same hole, which is one intersection of the canvas further down to the right from the point where the first group of stitches ended. Three more stitches are now put in on each side of the leaf. They are worked in groups of two, which go down into the same hole, and they are separated from each other by one thread of the canvas. A final diagonal stitch over three intersections of the canvas is put in to cover the holes into which these last three groups of two stitches go down.

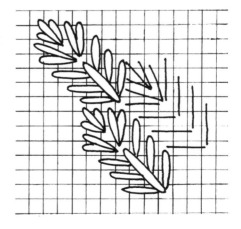

Leaf, Interlocking. See Interlocking Leaf

Leviathan. See Islamic and Smyrna

Link Surface

A vertical straight stitch is worked over four
horizontal threads of the canvas. The needle is
then brought out one vertical thread to the right
of the top of this stitch, and the working yarn
is taken under the stitch and brought back over
it to go down into the hole in the canvas one
vertical thread to the right of the bottom end of
the stitch. It makes a good filling stitch and can
be useful for over-stitching. The photograph
shows various ways of working this stitch.

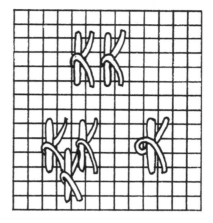

Can be used as an ornamental stitch onto a background of
Tent Stitch

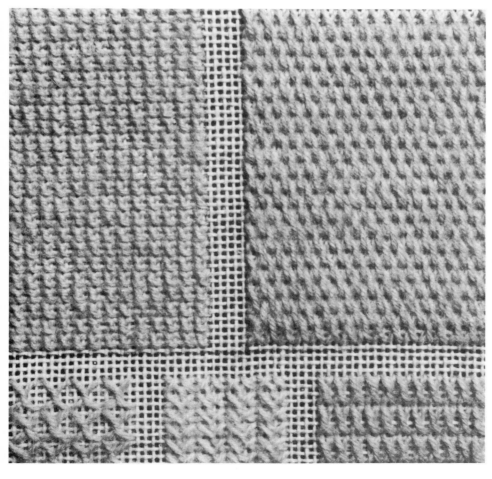

Linked — Straight and Half-drop

Four or more vertical straight stitches are taken over any even number of horizontal threads of the canvas, and one horizontal straight stitch is taken across the centre of each block of stitches.

As the diagrams show, this stitch can be worked either straight across the canvas horizontally or as a half-drop pattern diagonally.

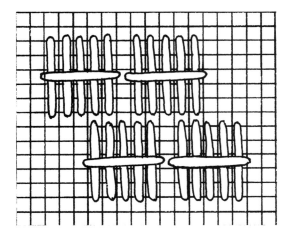

Five threads linked Straight Stitch

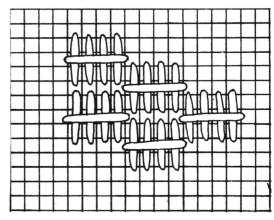

Four threads linked Half-drop

Long-armed Cross. See Long-Legged Cross

Long-legged Cross (Also known as Long-armed Cross, Plaited Slav and Greek)

This stitch is shown in the diagram as being worked over four horizontal threads of the canvas, but it can be worked over any number of threads. Each row begins with the working of a cross stitch. Then the needle is brought out of the hole at the bottom left-hand corner of the cross stitch, and the yarn is taken up obliquely over four horizontal and eight vertical threads of the canvas to the right. It is brought out again four horizon-

tal threads of the canvas immediately below this point, and an oblique stitch is put in up over four horizontal and four vertical threads of the canvas to the left. The process is continued by bringing out the needle four horizontal threads immediately below and repeating the sequence, but without the initial cross stitch. The diagram also shows the stitch worked diagonally.

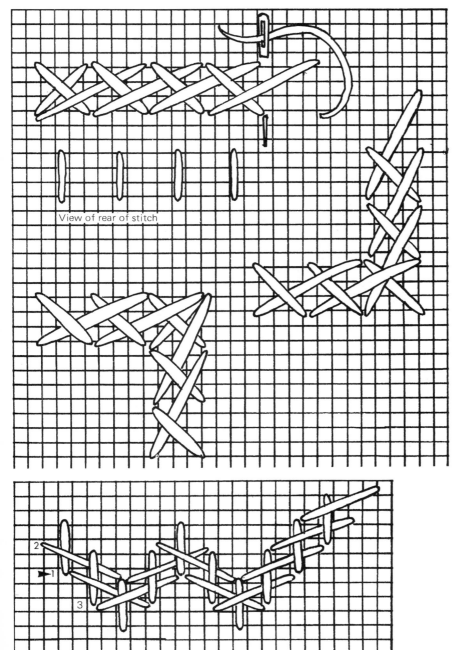

View of rear of stitch

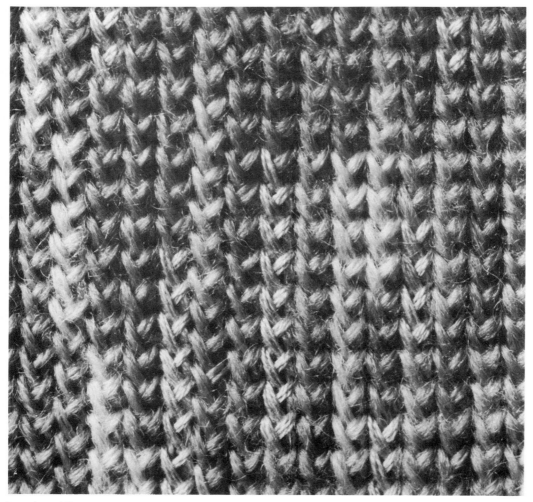

Long-legged Cross

Long-tailed Chain. See Chain, Long-tailed

Maltese Cross (Also known as Interlacing Stitch)

This is an interlacing stitch, which is based on a foundation of Double Herringbone Stitch. The diagram clearly shows the layout of the foundation stitches and also the method of interlacing.

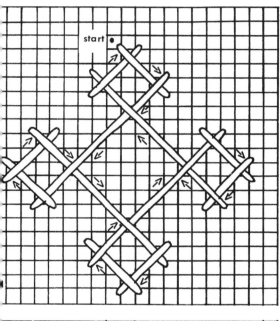

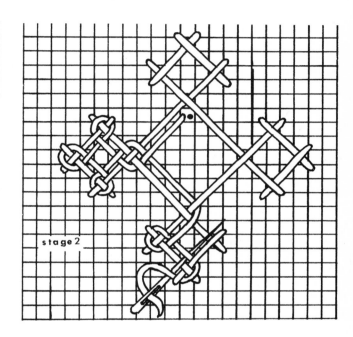

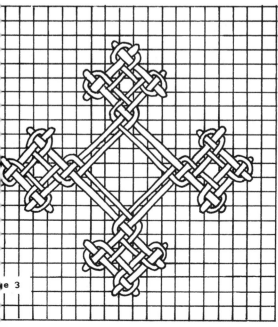

Milanese

This attractive stitch is worked in rows diagonally across the canvas, generally from top left to bottom right of the area to be covered. It consists of four individual stitches worked diagonally, the first over one intersection, the second over two, the third over three and the fourth over four intersections of the canvas, so that they form a small triangular shape. The working of these shapes continues along the diagonal, and then the next row of triangles is put in in reverse, so that they fit exactly together with the first row, as shown in the diagram, the longest stitch in one triangle always coming next to the shortest in the next triangle.

This stitch can also be worked as a series of back stitches, proceeding diagonally from bottom left to top right of an area of canvas. The first row consists of stitches taken alternately over one and

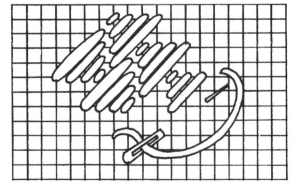

four intersections of the canvas; the second row passes alternately over two and three intersections; the third over three and two and the fourth over four and one. The whole process is then repeated, until the required area is covered.

Milanese Pinwheel. See Pinwheel, Milanese

Milanese Straight

In this form of Milanese Stitch the triangles of stitches are constructed of five horizontal straight stitches, taken respectively over two, four, six, eight and ten vertical threads of the canvas, and a row of these triangles is worked from top to bottom of the area to be covered. The second row is worked from bottom to top, with the position of the triangles reversed, so that the smallest stitch is placed beside the longest in the first row and the triangles fit exactly together.

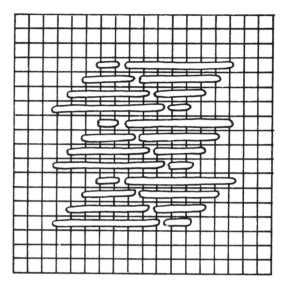

Milanese Straight — Variation

In this version of Milanese Straight Stitch triangular shapes, worked in horizontal straight stitches, alternate with triangles which are part of a large Eye Stitch. First of all in a row of stitches, worked from left to right across the canvas, a triangle formed from part of the Eye Stitch is put in. Eleven stitches are worked from adjacent holes in the canvas along the top edge of the area to be covered, and these eleven stitches all go down over six horizontal threads of the canvas into the centre hole. A Straight Milanese Stitch, formed of six horizontal stitches, which are worked respectively over two, four, six, eight, ten and twelve vertical threads of the canvas, is placed beside this first stitch in the row. The diagram shows how these triangular shapes are fitted together.

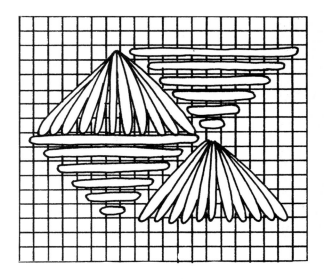

Mock Cretan

This stitch commences, as does Cretan Variation, with a small stitch over just one vertical thread of the canvas, which is tied down by two small vertical stitches over one horizontal thread, which are placed one on each side of the centre vertical thread. The next stitch starts from the hole in the canvas, which is one vertical thread to the left of the first stitch, and is taken down into the hole one vertical thread to the right of it, leaving the yarn slack, so that it can be tied down in a similar manner by means of two small vertical stitches over one horizontal thread, placed one horizontal thread immediately below the similar stitches tying down the first stitch. The third main stitch is started one intersection of the canvas down to the left of the left-hand end of the last stitch and finishes one intersection down to the right of its right-hand end, the yarn being tied down in a similar manner by the two small vertical stitches. The fourth main stitch in the group extends

from a point one vertical thread of the canvas to the left of the last main stitch to a point one vertical thread to the right of it, and the loop of the yarn is tied down in a similar way. Four more exactly similar individual main stitches are now put in beneath this last stitch, in order to complete the group, as shown in the diagram. Further groups of stitches are worked, as shown in the diagram, and further pairs of vertical straight stitches over one or two horizontal threads are put in to cover the unworked threads left between the groups of stitches.

The photograph shows the stitch worked as described above and also indicates how it can be developed by the addition of another long stitch, which is taken from the same holes in the canvas as the second main stitch in the group, and has the loop of the yarn tied down by two more similar small vertical stitches at the bottom of the group of stitches.

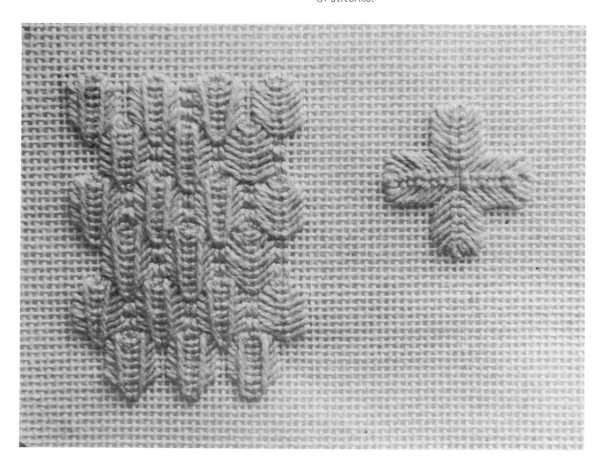

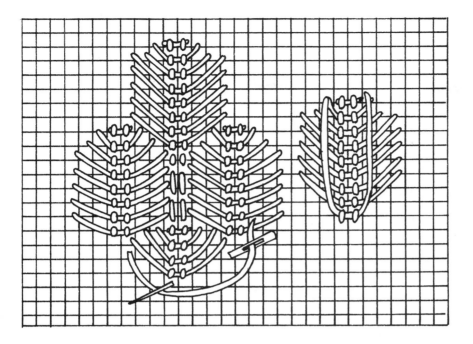

Montenegrin (Also known as Two-sided Stitch)

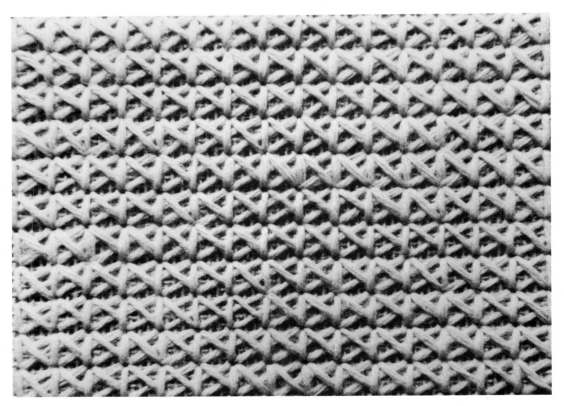

This stitch, which is worked from left to right, commences with a long diagonal stitch from the bottom left-hand corner, which is taken up over eight vertical and four horizontal threads of the canvas to the top right-hand corner of the stitch. The needle is then brought out at a point four horizontal threads down and four vertical threads back to the left, and the working yarn is taken up over four intersections of the canvas to the top left-hand corner of the stitch. The needle is again brought out at the same hole at the base of the stitch, from which it previously emerged, and a vertical straight stitch is taken up over four horizontal threads. Finally the needle is once more brought out at the same hole at the base of the stitch, ready to commence the next complete stitch in the row. The diagram shows the method of working the stitch, with the sequence of the individual stitches numbered.

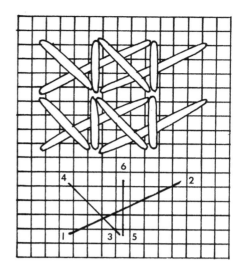

Montenegrin — Variation

A rather fuller version of Montenegrin Stitch is shown in the diagram, where the order of working the individual stitches is numbered. It begins in the same way as the simpler version with a long diagonal stitch from the bottom left-hand corner, which is taken up over eight vertical and four horizontal threads of the canvas to the top right-hand corner of the stitch. Then the needle is brought out at a point which is two horizontal threads of the canvas immediately above where the first stitch was begun, and a second diagonal stitch is put in up to the right over four vertical and two horizontal threads. The needle is again brought out at the bottom left-hand corner, and a third diagonal stitch is taken up over four vertical and four horizontal threads of the canvas to the right, to the same point where the second stitch ended. For the fourth stitch the needle is

brought out four horizontal threads immediately below this point, and the yarn is taken up to the left over four intersections of the canvas to the top left-hand corner of the stitch. Once more the needle is brought out at the same hole at the base of the last stitch, and the fifth and final stitch in the group, a vertical straight stitch over four horizontal threads, is put in. After working this stitch, the needle is again brought out at the same hole at the base, where it is ready to begin the next sequence of stitches.

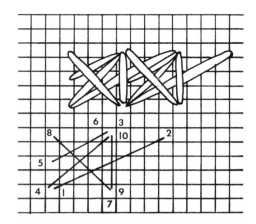

Moorish

This stitch is actually a version of Cushion Stitch, which is worked in rows diagonally across the canvas, the individual rows being separated from one another by diagonal rows of tent stitch. Each stitch consists of four diagonal stitches, worked respectively over one, two, three, two intersections of the canvas. It is a very useful stitch for filling large areas and is reasonably quick to work.

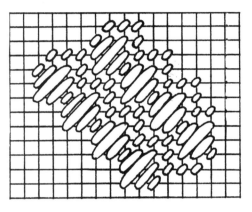

Mosaic

This is a very neat and attractive square stitch which, when worked, closely resembles in effect a small cross stitch. It is useful for backgrounds and can be successfully employed for shading. Each stitch consists of a group of three diagonal stitches worked over two horizontal and two vertical threads of the canvas, the first stitch over one intersection of the canvas, the second over two intersections and the third over one. It is, in fact, two tent stitches with one stitch taken over two intersections of the canvas placed in between them.

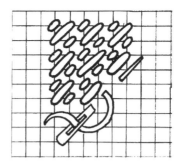

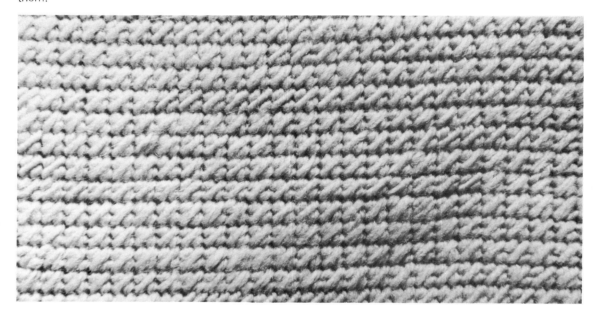

Mosaic — Reversed

This is an example of Mosaic Stitch in which alternate groups of three diagonal stitches are worked in the normal way from bottom left to top right, whereas the other groups in a row are worked from bottom right to top left.

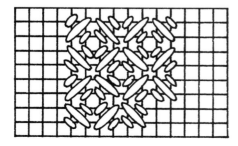

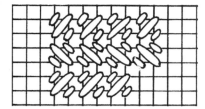

Mosaic-Reversed Variation

Mosaic Tile

This stitch consists of a normal Mosaic Stitch, worked over two horizontal and two vertical threads of the canvas, which is surrounded by four straight stitches — each over four threads of the canvas — so that it is enclosed within a square. When the first straight stitch of the second group of stitches is being worked, the yarn comes out of the same hole as the straight stitch of the first group. This is shown clearly in the diagram.

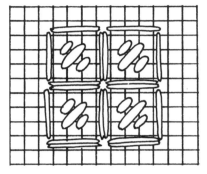

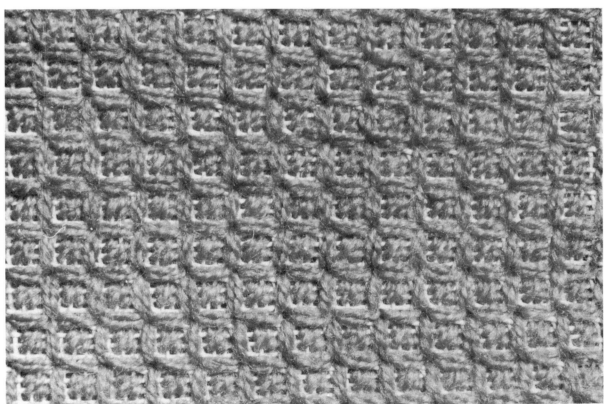

Multiplait. See Herringbone Squared

Norwich (Also known as Waffle Stitch)

This stitch is best worked with a tightly spun, non-hairy yarn. It can be worked in various sizes, provided it covers a square with an uneven number of threads of the canvas. The diagram shows the individual stitches, numbered in order of working. It will be noticed that the method of working follows a regular pattern, until the last stitch is put in, when the needle is slipped under instead of over stitch 29-30, the last stitch it passes before entering the canvas at hole 36.

Norwich Stitch can be worked over an even number of threads of the canvas, but it then means that the final stitches will go into the same hole in the canvas on each side of the square, without crossing over one another.

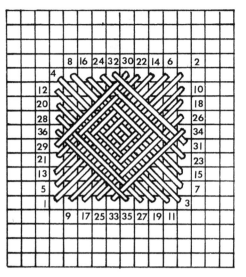

Oblique Slav. See Gobelin Oblique

Oblong Cross. See Cross, Oblong

Oblong Cross — Double-tied. See Cross, Oblong — Double-tied

Oblong Cross — Half-drop. See Cross, Oblong — Half-drop

Oblong Cross Overlaid. See Cross Overlaid, Oblong

Octagonal Eye

This eyelet is formed by working eight stitches into a centre hole in the canvas. Each individual stitch is over three threads of the canvas, and two threads are left between the stitches where they meet the perimeter of the octagonal shape. Back stitches are worked over these two threads between the individual stitches, and another back stitch is placed in the space between two octagonal eyelets, when they are fitted in together, as shown in the diagram.

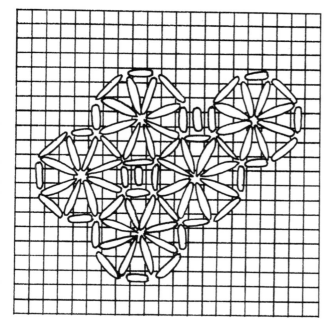

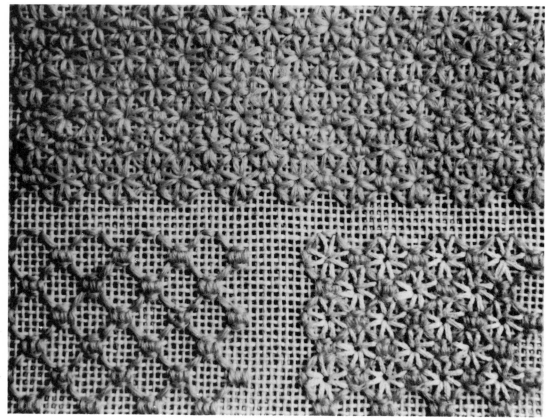

Octagonal Eye

Old English Knot. See Palestrina

Old Parisian. See Florentine

One-sided

This stitch should be worked in horizontal rows from right to left. It begins with a cross stitch over three vertical and three horizontal threads of the canvas. The yarn is then brought out at the bottom left-hand corner of the cross, and a long oblique stitch is taken up over six horizontal and three vertical threads of the canvas to the right, to a point three horizontal threads directly above the top right-hand corner of the cross. From that point the needle is brought out three vertical threads directly to the left, and the yarn is taken down to the right across the long stitch and into the hole at the top right-hand corner of the cross. The needle is brought out again at a point just one vertical thread of the canvas to the right of the top of the last stitch, and another oblique stitch is taken down to the right over the long stitch to a point one intersection of the canvas up to the right of the top right-hand corner of the cross. From this point the needle is brought out at a point three vertical threads directly to the left of the top left-hand corner of the initial cross stitch,

and a second cross stitch is now worked beside the first one, but in reversed position, and the needle is then brought out at the top left-hand corner of the second cross, and another long oblique stitch is taken down to the right over six horizontal and three vertical threads of the canvas, finishing three horizontal threads directly below the bottom right-hand corner of the second cross. The needle is then brought out three vertical threads directly back to the left, and a stitch is taken up over the second long stitch and into the same hole as the bottom right-hand corner of second cross. The needle then comes out again one vertical thread to the right of the bottom end of the last stitch, and another stitch is taken up to the right across the second long stitch to a point one intersection of the canvas down to the right from the bottom right-hand corner of the second cross stitch. Finally the needle comes out three vertical threads of the canvas directly to the left of the bottom left-hand corner of the second cross, where it is ready to start the whole sequence of stitches again.

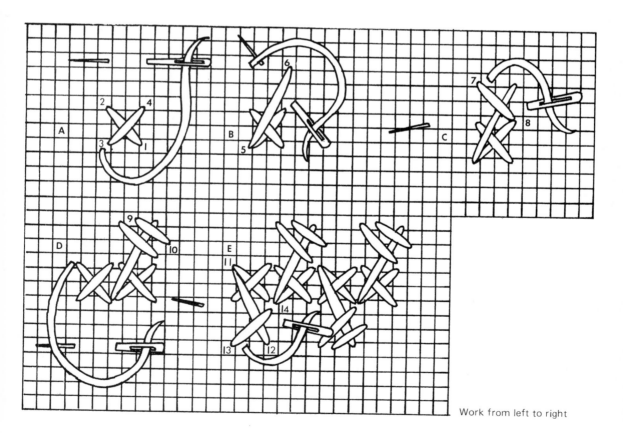

Work from left to right

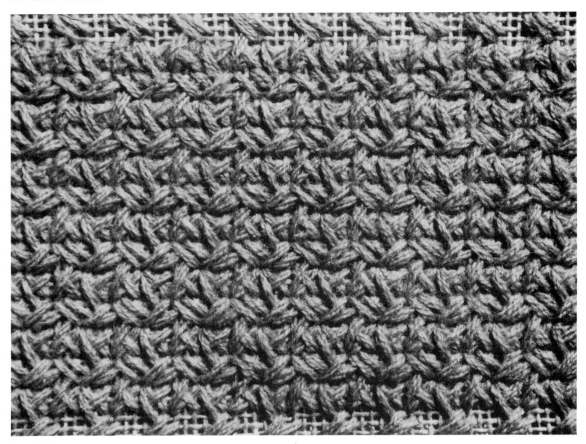

One-sided

Open Buttonhole Filling. See Buttonhole
Filling, Open

Oriental

This stitch is worked from the top left to the
bottom right. Four diagonal stitches are worked
respectively over one, two, three and four intersections of the canvas, so that they form a triangular shape. The small stitch, which starts a new
group, is worked over the central intersection
immediately below the previous long stitch. The
process of constructing the triangular shapes is
continued diagonally across to the bottom edge
of the area to be covered. On the return journey
the groups of stitches are reversed, with the long
stitches emerging from the same holes in the
canvas as the long stitches in the previous row. The
three vertical and two horizontal threads of the
canvas, which are left uncovered between the
rows of triangular shapes, are now worked over
with three diagonal stitches, each one over two
intersections of the canvas. These stitches slope
in the same direction as those in the triangular
groups. As in the case of Milanese Stitch, which

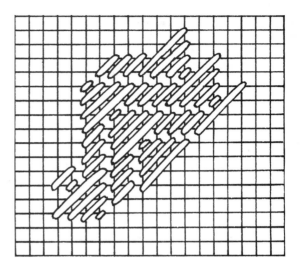

it closely resembles, a large area of this stitch
needs to be worked to show its full beauty.

Outline Stitch. See Stem

Overlaid

This stitch with its use of an overlaid yarn can
give an interesting texture to a piece of work.
Upright crosses over eight vertical and eight
horizontal threads of the canvas are worked first
across the area to be covered. Then a diagonal
stitch is put in, going up to the right over four
intersections of the canvas from the centre of
each cross and also from the foot of each cross,
as is shown in the diagram. After this stage has
been completed, diagonal stitches over two intersections of the canvas are then worked from the
top left to the bottom right of the area and crossing the centre of each of the upright crosses.
Finally one horizontal stitch and one vertical
stitch, each over six threads of the canvas, are
put in at right-angles to one another on top of the
upright cross stitches, as shown in the diagram.
The overlaid stitches should be worked in a yarn
of contrasting colour to that used for working
the initial upright cross stitches.

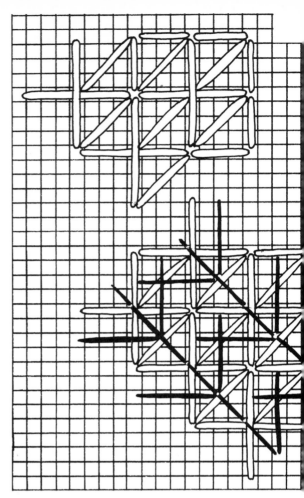

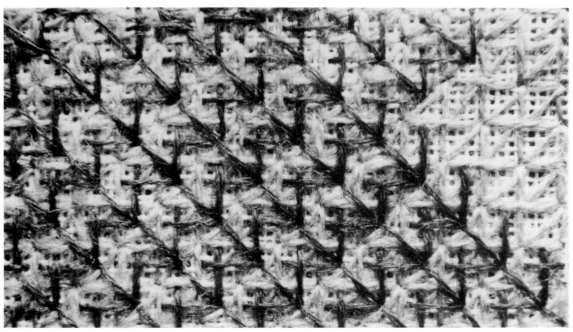

Palestrina (Also known as Old English Knot, Double Knot or Tied Coral)

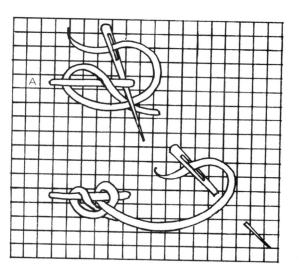

This stitch should be commenced at the left-hand side of the area to be worked. The yarn is brought up through the canvas at point A (see diagram), and a horizontal straight stitch is taken over six vertical threads of the canvas. The needle is brought out at a point two intersections of the canvas down to the right, and the yarn is taken up over the long horizontal stitch by passing the needle down behind this stitch. Then the yarn should be held down with the thumb, whilst the needle is passed down behind the long stitch a second time and is brought out over the loop of the yarn, as in buttonholing. The next stitch covers six vertical threads of the canvas directly to the right and begins the process all over again.

If it proves necessary to do so, the length of the individual stitches may be varied.

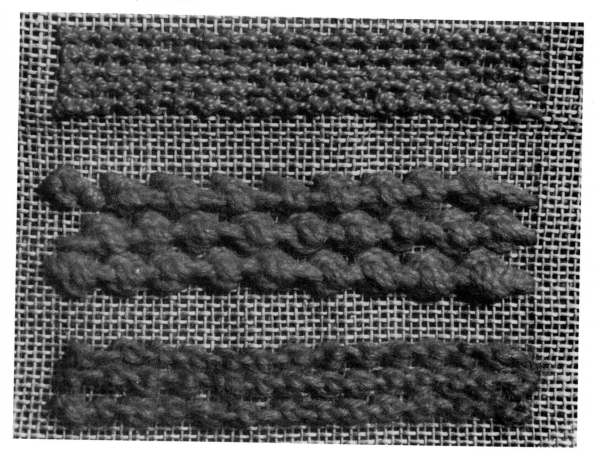

Parisian

This is a vertical straight stitch similar to Hungarian Stitch, but it is worked over two and four horizontal threads of the canvas only, with the sequence being repeated indefinitely and no threads of canvas left uncovered between the groups of two vertical stitches. It is essential, when working straight vertical stitches, that the yarn should be thick enough to cover the canvas completely.

When this stitch is worked diagonally, it is sometimes known as Small Diagonal Stitch.

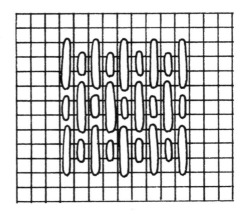

Parisian — Stepped

This variation of Parisian Stitch is worked from left to right across the canvas. The first row of stitches consists of one vertical straight stitch over two horizontal threads of the canvas, followed by one stitch over four horizontal threads and three more stitches over two horizontal threads. This sequence is repeated to the end of the row. The second row starts with one vertical stitch over four canvas threads, which is placed directly under the first small stitch in the row above. This is followed by one stitch over two horizontal threads, which comes under the first long stitch in the first row, then another long stitch over four horizontal threads, followed by a short stitch over two threads. This is repeated to the end of the row. The third row consists of three short

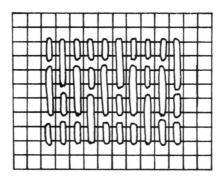

stitches over two horizontal canvas threads, followed by one long stitch over four horizontal threads, with this sequence being repeated to the end of the row.

Part Eye with Cross

This square stitch is worked over six threads of
the canvas. One stitch over three intersections is
taken from each corner of the square into the
centre hole. Then on either side of these first
four diagonal stitches other stitches are worked,
starting one thread from the corners along all the
sides of the square, and going down into the centre
hole. The space left between the groups of stitches
is filled with an upright Cross Stitch.

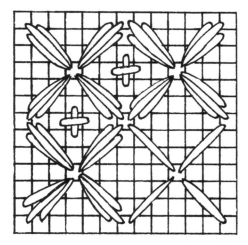

Pekinese (Sometimes known as Chinese Stitch)

A line of back stitches, each one over a predetermined number of vertical threads of the canvas, is worked across the area to be covered. Then a yarn of the same or of a contrasting colour is laced under and over this row of back stitches, as shown in the diagram. Pekinese Stitch can be used as a linear stitch or as a filling stitch.

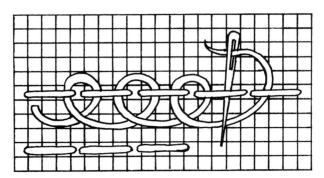

Petal

This is a square stitch, which is worked over ten canvas threads. A diagonal stitch is taken from each corner of the square down into the centre hole, and then two more oblique stitches are worked from the two holes in the canvas on each side of each of these first stitches and they are also taken down into the centre hole. The yarn is then brought up to the surface at a point one thread of the canvas away from the centre hole and beneath one of the groups of stitches already worked. It is wound around the centre hole five times, passing under the other groups of stitches on the way, and the outer ring of the five is then tied down with a back stitch at top and bottom and on both sides of the square.

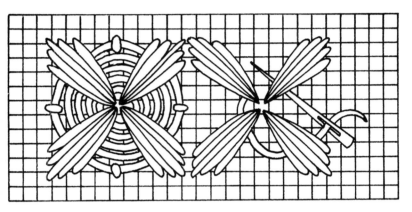

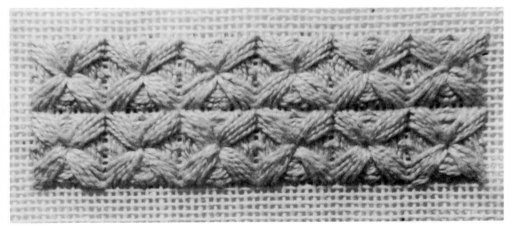

Petal — Variation

The only difference between this variation and the original Petal Stitch is that it is worked over eleven canvas threads instead of ten, which means that all the stitches do not go down into the same centre hole, but each corner group goes down into its own hole beside the centre of the square, where one horizontal and one vertical thread of the canvas are left uncovered. The yarn is still wound around the centre five times, but in this version the outer ring of the five is tied down with two back stitches instead of one, and areas of two vertical and five horizontal threads or five vertical and two horizontal threads of the canvas are left uncovered between groups of stitches. These latter areas can be worked over with a contrasting yarn, and a tent stitch or small cross stitch can be used to cover the centre.

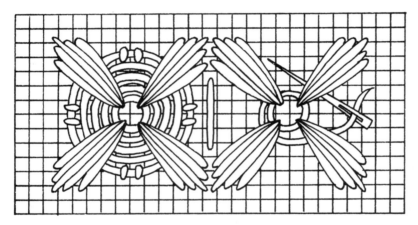

Petit Point. See Tent

Picot

In the photograph this stitch is shown worked over three horizontal and three vertical threads of the canvas, but it can be worked larger, if so required. A cross stitch over three intersections of the canvas is worked first. The yarn is then brought out at a point one horizontal thread of the canvas below the top left-hand corner of the cross, and, whilst a loop of the yarn is held on the surface, the needle is slipped down under the cross stitch from the top and out through the loop of the yarn, as shown in the diagram. The loop is then pulled tight, and the yarn is woven back over one and under two legs of the cross. This process of weaving over and under the legs of the cross, including the extra stitch which was formed on the side line at the start, is continued around the cross for as many times as it is possible to pass the yarn through, and the Picot is forced up as high as possible. It is necessary to make sure that the initial cross stitch is tightly tensioned.

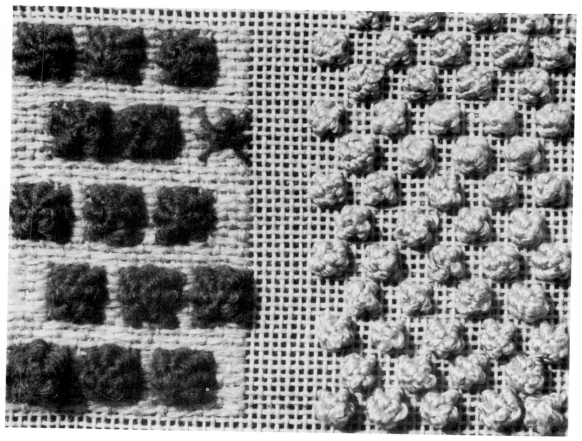

Pineapple

Four vertical straight stitches over four horizontal threads of the canvas are worked first. A cross stitch, extending over four horizontal and five vertical threads of the canvas, is then put in over the top of these four straight stitches. This cross stitch is finally tied down in the centre by means of a small diagonal stitch over the central vertical thread of canvas.

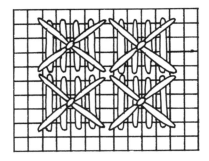

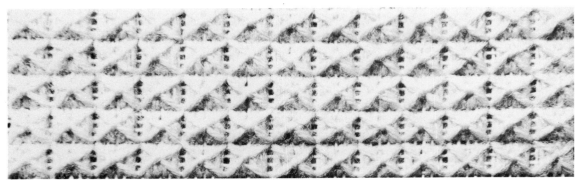

Pineapple — Half-drop

When Pineapple Stitch is worked diagonally, the finished appearance which it presents is quite different from the way it appears, when it is worked in vertical or horizontal rows. Each group of stitches, when worked diagonally, drops down two horizontal threads of the canvas lower than the group before it.

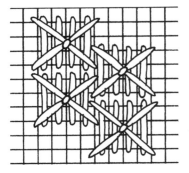

Pinwheel, Milanese

This attractive stitch is formed by working groups of Milanese Stitch around a centre point to give the appearance of a revolving catherine-wheel.

Isolated pinwheels can be worked in conjunction with other stitches, or they can be used as an all-over pattern.

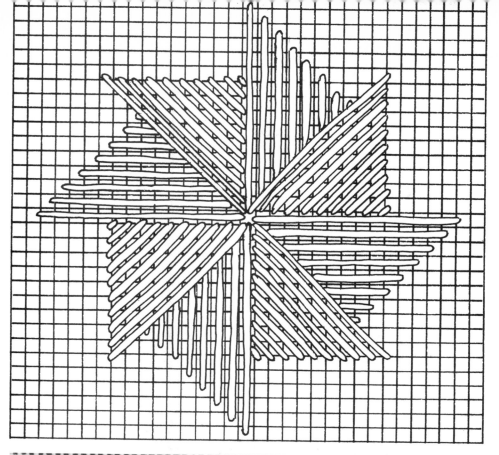

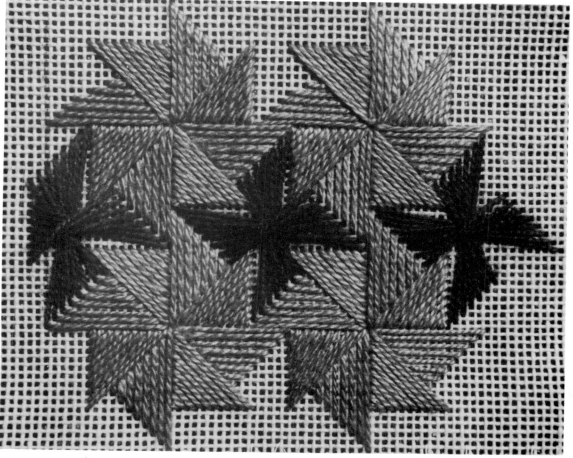

Plaited

This stitch is very similar to Fern Stitch, except that the vertical rows of stitches overlap one another by one thread of the canvas. This gives to the finished work a closely interwoven appearance, which is rather like knitting. See diagram and the photograph. The diagram also shows that, although this stitch is normally worked in vertical rows downwards, it can be worked in rows horizontally.

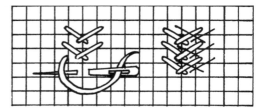

Plaited Stitch worked vertically

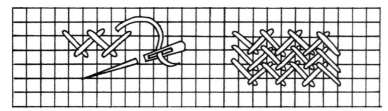

Plaited Stitch worked horizontally

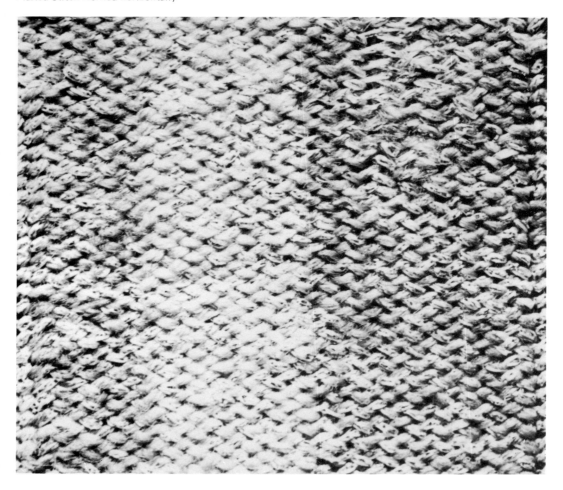

Plaited Cross

A cross stitch is first worked over four intersections of the canvas. The yarn is then brought out one horizontal thread immediately above the bottom left-hand corner of this stitch and is taken over both legs of the cross to the same point above the bottom right-hand corner. It is then passed under the bottom right-hand leg of the cross, without entering the canvas, and is brought up over both legs of the cross to the top right-hand corner. Passing over and under the legs of the cross in this way, the yarn is taken right round the square and comes back to the bottom left-hand corner, where it passes under the first stitch that was put in over this leg, as well as passing under the leg of the cross itself, before going down into the hole in the canvas from which it first emerged.

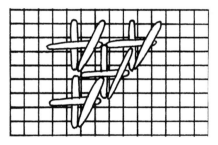

Plaited Slav (See also Long-legged Cross)

This stitch is based on an upright cross stitch, worked over four vertical and four horizontal threads of the canvas. After the upright cross has been worked, the yarn is brought up at the base of the cross, from the same hole as the vertical stitch came from, and an oblique stitch is taken up over four horizontal threads of the canvas and two vertical threads to the right, crossing over the right-hand end of the horizontal bar of the cross.

Worked over four canvas threads

Worked over four threads
Work left to right downwards

Worked over two canvas threads

Plaited Square

This square stitch is generally worked in rows diagonally across the canvas from top left to bottom right, each square dropping down by one horizontal canvas thread below the previous stitch. The square is formed by taking a vertical stitch up over four horizontal threads of the canvas and crossing it with a horizontal stitch over four vertical threads, starting from a point one intersection of the canvas down to the left from the top of the first stitch. This second stitch is then similarly crossed by working another vertical stitch over four horizontal threads, and the fourth and final stitch, a horizontal one over four vertical threads, is then taken over stitch number three, but under stitch number one.

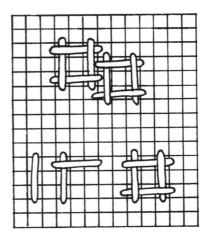

Plaited Square Diagonal

The diagram shows the working of the diagonal version.

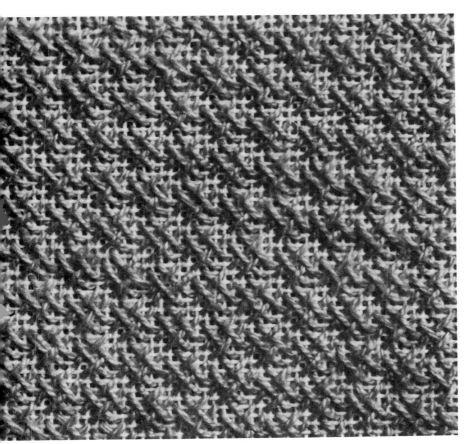

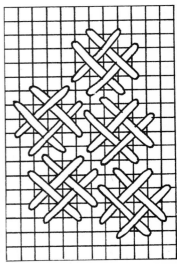

Point de Sable. See Back

Ponto Rosinhas. See Brazilian

Porto Rico Rose. See Bullion

Portuguese Filling

This stitch is worked over a series of horizontal stitches, which are put in first over the area to be covered. The diagram shows these horizontal bars, each one of which extends over seven vertical threads of the canvas. They are arranged in vertical rows with three horizontal threads of the canvas left uncovered between the individual stitches. Over this foundation Stem Stitch is then worked, starting from the bottom and working upwards. To begin the working four vertical straight stitches are put in over the first two horizontal bars from a point two horizontal threads down from the first bar. Then two Stem Stitches are worked over and under the second and third bars without going down through the canvas, the process being continued to the top of the row, as shown in the diagram.

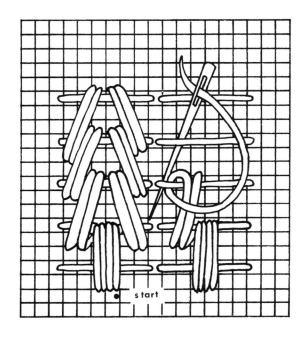

Portuguese Stem

This stitch is normally worked on linen, but it can also be used quite successfully on canvas. It is an exceedingly beautiful stitch to use where a knotted, slightly raised line is needed.

The working of the stitch is completed in three movements. It starts with an ordinary stem stitch, worked over one vertical and four horizontal threads of the canvas, with the needle being brought out two threads down and one to the left, as shown in A in the diagram. The needle is then slipped under the first stitch from right to left, as at B in the diagram, and the yarn is wrapped round the stitch and tightened. The process of wrapping the yarn round the stitch is then repeated, keeping the second coil just below the first (C).

A second stitch is put in by entering the needle two horizontal threads of the canvas above the top end of the first stitch and bringing it out again two threads down and one vertical thread to the

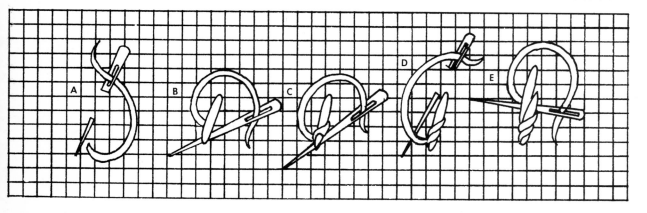

left of the first stitch (D). The needle is then taken
under the top part of the first stitch and the
bottom part of the second stitch, and the yarn is
wrapped round the stitch as before to make two
coils, one beneath the other (E).

Post. See Bullion

Quick

Long lines of yarn are 'laid' across the area to be
worked. It is essential that these 'laid' threads
accurately follow the intersections of the canvas.
These lines are then crossed at regular intervals by
groups of three diagonal stitches over five intersections of the canvas, worked at right angles to
the 'laid' threads. See the diagram for the spacing.

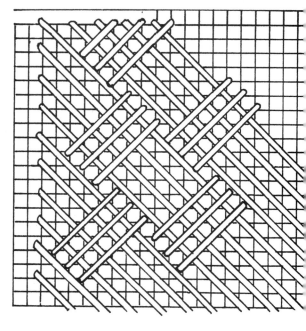

Quodlibet

A long vertical straight stitch is taken down over
twelve horizontal threads of the canvas. The
needle is brought out at a point one vertical thread
to the left of this long stitch and six horizontal
threads down from the top end. A stitch is taken
from this point down into the hole in the canvas
at the bottom end of the long stitch, and another
similar stitch is taken from a point one further
vertical thread to the left and down into the same
hole in the canvas. These two stitches are repeated
on the right-hand side of the long stitch to form
the bottom 'arrow-head'. Similar stitches are then
put in to form the top 'arrow-head', and a back
stitch across two vertical threads is worked in
the centre of the long stitch. The diagram shows
how these stitches can be fitted together to cover
an area of the canvas.

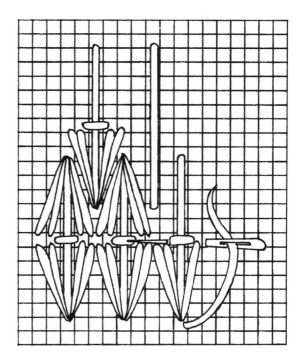

Radiating

Triangular shapes are formed by five straight stitches radiating from the same hole in the canvas. In a row of such groups of stitches, worked from left to right across the canvas, the groups alternate between having the common centre hole on the left and having it on the right. Adjacent rows of triangular shapes are arranged to fit together, so that they cover the canvas. If it is necessary to cover the canvas more thoroughly, a back stitch can be worked over two horizontal threads of the canvas at the point where the groups of stitches meet.

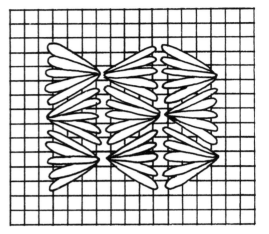

Raised Chain Band

Before beginning to work the individual stitches, a foundation of horizontal straight stitches over four vertical threads of the canvas is worked from top to bottom of the area to be covered, each horizontal stitch being placed two horizontal threads immediately below the one above it.

The needle is then brought out at the centre hole just one horizontal thread above the top horizontal stitch, and the working yarn is taken over and then back under this stitch to the left, to be brought round over it in a loop, whilst the needle

is again taken under it on the right and brought out through the loop of the yarn, where it is ready to begin the second stitch. Only the basic horizontal stitches are taken through the canvas; the knotted part of each stitch is worked on the surface. The second row of stitches can either be placed directly side by side with the first row or be worked with a half-drop, when individual stitches may be fitted into the spaces between stitches in the first row. The diagram also shows how this stitch may be worked diagonally across the canvas.

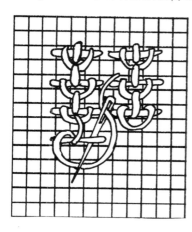 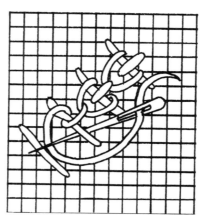 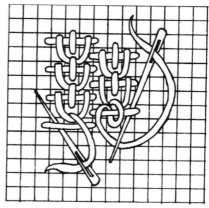

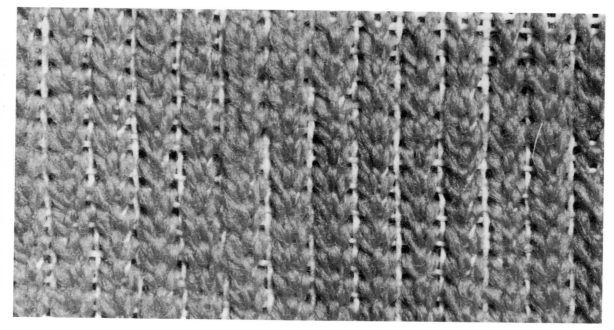

Raised Spot

This stitch is worked over four horizontal threads of the canvas. The yarn is taken into the same hole top and bottom as many times as is possible, in order to get a really hard, raised effect. This can mean as many as twenty times or more, depending on the thickness of the yarn.

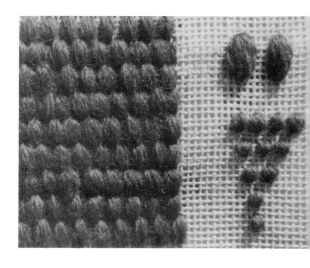

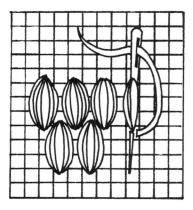

Ray. See Fan

Renaissance

This stitch is worked in groups of four vertical stitches, each individual stitch over two horizontal threads of the canvas. The working yarn must be of the correct thickness to suit the mesh of the canvas, in order that it may fully cover it. The diagram shows the position of the needle at different stages of the working. The photograph shows the stitch worked in the normal way and as a half-drop.

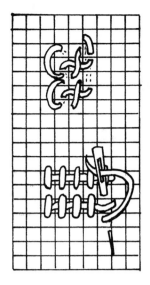

Renaissance Tied. See French Variation

Rep (Also known as Aubusson Stitch)

This is a stitch which must be worked on double-thread (Penelope) canvas. Two small stitches are worked over each intersection of the double canvas. To begin the stitch the double horizontal thread is split, and the yarn is brought up between the threads and is taken diagonally up and over one double intersection of the canvas to the right. The needle is then brought back down under the double intersection to the left, and the second small stitch is put in up over the double vertical thread to the right and down between the two horizontal threads of the canvas. Care must be taken to choose a working yarn of the correct thickness to ensure that the canvas will be adequately covered.

Worked on double mesh — Penelope canvas

Rhodes

This is a bulky square stitch, which may be worked over any number of threads of the canvas from a minimum of three horizontal and three vertical threads. The working consists of taking a stitch, which passes over the centre of the square, into every hole around the sides of the square, beginning with a stitch from the hole one vertical thread to the right of the bottom left-hand corner, which is taken down into the hole one vertical thread to the left of the top right-hand corner of the square, and progressing right round the square, always proceeding in the same direction, to finish with a diagonal stitch from the top right-hand corner to the bottom left-hand corner of the square. If the stitch being worked is a very large one, then it is a good idea to take a long stitch across the corners, after the main square stitch has been completed, or a small stitch can tie it down in the centre. Such extra stitches across the corners can only be successfully introduced, however, when the completed Rhodes Stitch covers an even number of threads of the canvas.

Worked on an uneven number of canvas threads

Worked over an even number of threads

Rhodes Half Half-drop

This stitch is worked in rows diagonally down across the area of canvas to be covered. It is, as the name implies, just half a normal Rhodes Stitch, and each group of stitches is started half its depth below the previous group. The diagram shows the stitch worked over six threads of the canvas. To begin the second group of stitches the needle is brought out three horizontal threads of the canvas below the bottom right-hand corner of the first group of stitches and two vertical threads to the left. In this way the second group of stitches is fitted closely beside the first group.

This is a very attractive stitch, which can be worked over any even number of threads of the canvas.

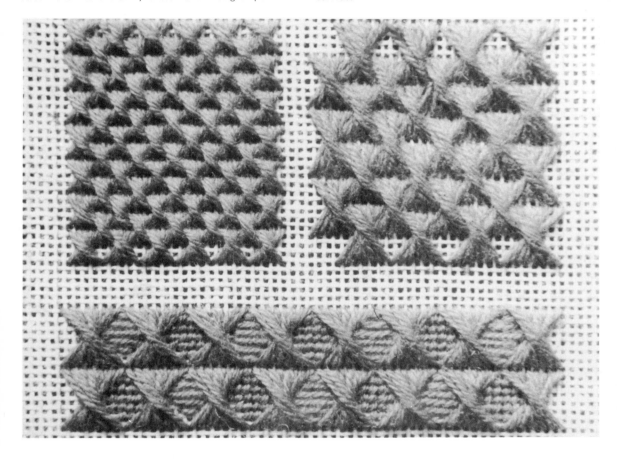

Rhodes — Half — Plaited

This stitch is similar in construction to Half Rhodes (Half-drop), but the rows of stitches are worked horizontally across the canvas. The first row is worked from left to right, and the sequence of the individual stitches is the same; but the second row is worked from right to left, and the sequence of the individual stitches is also from right to left. This means that in one row of stitches the top individual diagonal stitch in a group is inclined from bottom right to top left and in the next row from bottom left to top right.

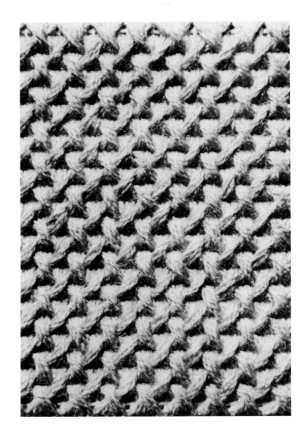

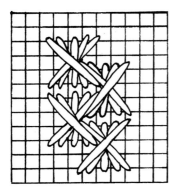

Rhodes — Octagonal

This stitch can only be worked over a multiple of four threads of the canvas. The diagram shows it worked over sixteen threads. The working is similar to that for ordinary Rhodes Stitch: seven stitches, which cross over the centre point, are worked from the holes along the base-line to those along the top edge of the octagon, the work proceeding from left to right; then four stitches are worked from the intersection of the canvas at the bottom right over to those at the top left; seven more stitches are put in from the right vertical side of the octagon over to the left side; and finally four more stitches from the intersections at the top right to those at the bottom left.

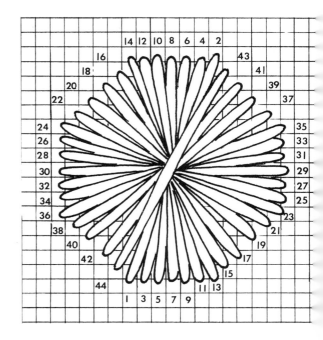

Over sixteen canvas threads

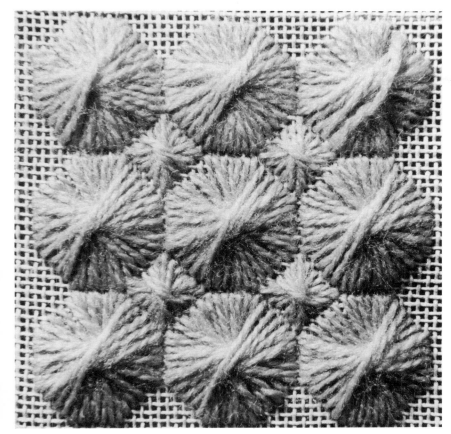

Over eight canvas threads

Rice (Also known as Crossed Corners)

This square stitch is begun by working a large diagonal cross stitch over an even number of threads of the canvas. The needle is then brought up through the hole in the centre of one side of the cross, and a back stitch is taken over the arm of the cross and down into the centre hole on the top edge of it. Once again the needle is brought up, this time thorugh the centre hole on the bottom edge of the cross stitch, and a small stitch is taken over an arm of the cross and down into the same hole from which the first small stitch started. The needle is then brought up at the centre hole on the opposite side of the cross stitch, and the yarn is taken back over an arm of the cross and into the same hole on the bottom edge, where the second small stitch started. Finally the needle is brought up through the centre hole on the top edge of the cross, and a stitch is taken over the fourth arm of the cross and into the hole on the side, where the third small stitch started.

In this way individual rice stitches can be worked, but, if it is desired to put in the small stitches in a contrasting colour, or with a different type of yarn, then a row of the basic cross stitches should be worked first, and the small stitches should be put in afterwards.

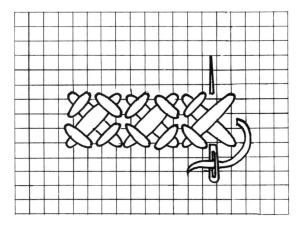

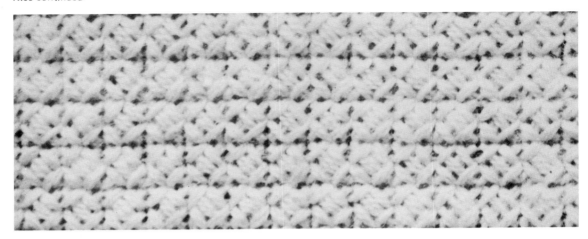

Rice — Elongated

This stitch is formed by working an oblong cross over six horizontal and two vertical threads of the canvas, and crossing the corners of the stitch with small oblique stitches over one vertical thread and three horizontal threads. It is best to work this stitch as a half-drop, taken diagonally down across the canvas. This method ensures maximum coverage of the canvas.

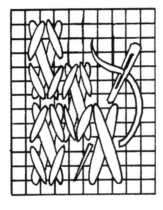

Rice — Multiple

This stitch is worked in the same way as Triple Rice, but it has two extra diagonal stitches, each over one intersection of the canvas, put in over the legs of the cross, making five such stitches in all. One of these extra stitches is worked at the centre of the cross and one over the tip of the leg in each case.

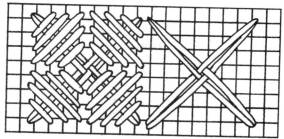

Rice — Straight

In working this straight version of Rice Stitch, an upright cross is taken over four vertical and four horizontal threads of the canvas, and a back stitch over two threads of the canvas is worked over the ends of the cross.

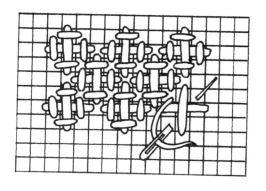

Rice — Triple

A diagonal cross stitch is worked over six threads of the canvas. As in normal Rice Stitch, diagonal stitches are taken from the centre hole at each side of the cross over the legs of the cross and down into the centre hole at the top and bottom edges of the cross. Two further diagonal stitches, each over two intersections of the canvas, are put in over each leg of the cross, one above and one below each of the first diagonal stitches.

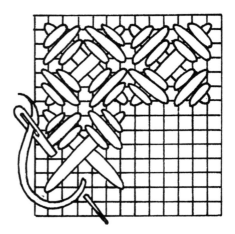

Rick-rack

This stitch is started by the working of a horizontal row of groups of two horizontal straight stitches over four vertical threads of the canvas. Then a vertical stitch over three horizontal threads is placed over the space between the groups of stitches. This is followed by the working of a diagonal stitch which commences one horizontal thread down from the bottom end of the first vertical stitch and enters the canvas again one horizontal thread above the top end of the second vertical stitch. A similar diagonal stitch is put in across the second group of two horizontal stitches, and the process is continued to the end of the row. On the return journey a diagonal stitch is worked, which commences one horizontal thread down from the bottom end of the last vertical stitch in the row and enters the canvas again one horizontal thread above the top end of the next-to-last

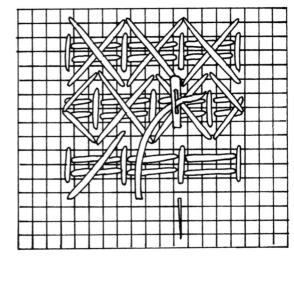

vertical stitch. This process is then continued
until the point one horizontal thread above the
first vertical stitch in the row is reached and each
group of two horizontal stitches has been covered
by a large diagonal cross stitch. Succeeding rows of
stitches are moved along to commence two vertical
threads to the right each time and three horizontal
threads further down, thus enabling the worker
to fit the groups of stitches in succeeding rows
really neatly into one another.

Ridge

This oblique cross stitch is worked in rows
proceeding downwards from the top left-hand
corner of the area to be covered. It starts with an
oblique stitch from a point two horizontal threads
below the top left-hand corner, and this stitch
is taken up over two horizontal and four vertical
threads of the canvas to the right. Over this
stitch a second one is worked, beginning one
horizontal thread below the point where the first
stitch started and one vertical thread to the right,
and finishing one horizontal thread above the end
of the first stitch and one vertical thread to the
left. The next cross starts at a point two horizontal
threads immediately below the start of the first
stitch. See the diagram.

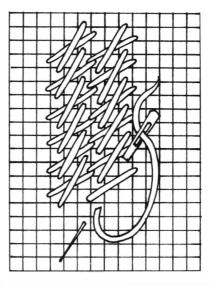

Ringed Square

This stitch is commenced by working a diagonal cross stitch over twelve threads of the canvas, with an upright cross of the same size worked on top of it. Then eight small oblique stitches over two and one threads of the canvas are worked from points on the outside edge of the square half-way between the large cross stitchs and pointing towards the centre of the cross. The needle is then brought out one hole below the centre and one to the left of the leg of the upright cross. The yarn is passed over the leg of the diagonal cross to the left, and then back under it and also under the leg of the upright cross to its right. It is then taken back to the left and over and under the leg of the upright cross, as well as going under the leg of the diagonal cross to the right. This process of passing the yarn over and under the legs of the crosses is continued right round several times, until the small oblique stitches are reached. These are then included in the

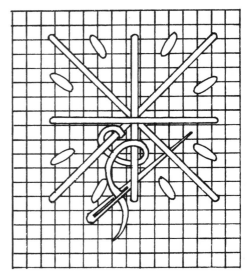

wrapping process, until the outer edge is reached, and the original crosses are completely covered, so that they form raised ridges.

Rococo

In this stitch an even number of vertical, straight stitches is worked by passing the yarn several times through the same two holes in the canvas, one of which is directly above the other and an unspecified number of threads of the canvas distant from it. The individual stitches are each tied down to a thread of the canvas, so as to produce a balanced effect. If the stitches pass over an even number of horizontal threads of the canvas, a back stitch should be used to tie them down, but, if they pass over an uneven number of threads, a tent stitch must be used to fix them. See the diagram.

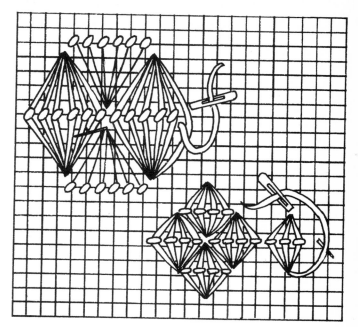

Rococo on single mesh canvas
Tie down with Tent Stitch if the threads are an uneven number
Tie down with Back Stitch if threads are an even number

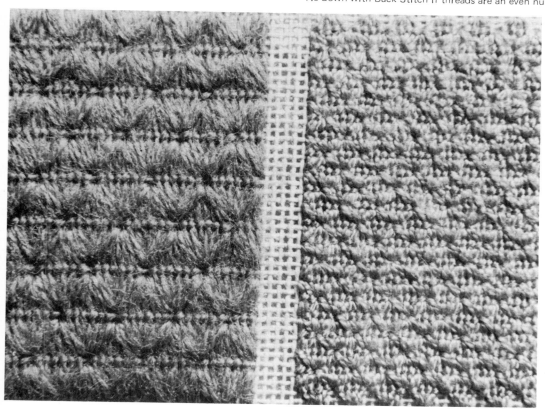

Worked on single mesh canvas

Rococo Square

This stitch is best worked on a coarse canvas or a double-thread canvas, as it is somewhat tedious to work, when a fine canvas is used. The photograph shows it worked on 16 single-mesh canvas. The groups of stitches are set in alternate squares, leaving the intervening squares open. There is a certain amount of preliminary work to be done first, when a fine canvas is used. Two vertical and two horizontal threads must be removed and darned back into the surrounding canvas to form the squares, and one thread must be left untouched for working over. The method of proceeding then is to work the blocks of stitches in rows diagonally across the canvas, as shown in the diagram.

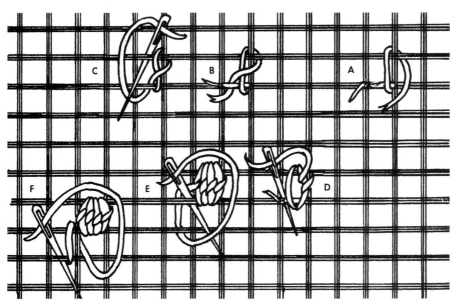

Rococo on double mesh canvas

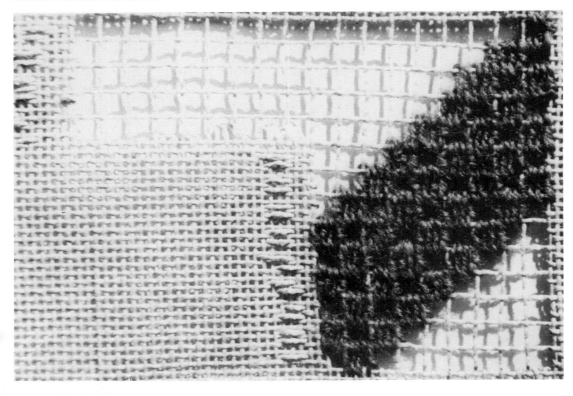

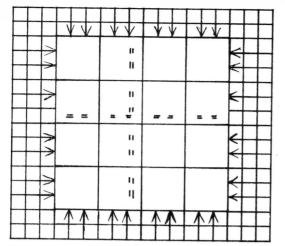 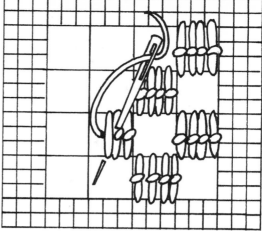

Cut and withdraw two horizontal and two vertical threads and fasten to back of canvas leaving one horizontal and one vertical thread between as indicated

Roll. See Bullion

Roman Filling

A group of seven vertical straight stitches is worked over two, four, six, eight, six, four and two horizontal threads of the canvas respectively. Each individual stitch is tied down by means of a back stitch over one vertical thread of the canvas. Rows of these stitches are worked horizontally across the area to be covered, with a space of one hole of the canvas being left between each group of stitches. Subsequent rows of these stitches are fitted into the spaces between groups of stitches in the row above, with the longest stitch worked into the centre hole between two groups.

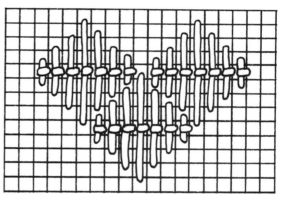

Rose

A Rice Stitch is worked over four threads of the canvas, and is then surrounded on all four sides with a group of five satin stitches, worked over four, six, eight, six and four threads of the canvas respectively. At each corner of the Rice Stitch, and between the blocks of satin stitches, a cross stitch is worked. The canvas threads which are left between the cross stitches can either be left unworked, as in the diagram, or another small rice stich can be worked over two vertical and two horizontal threads of the canvas to cover them.

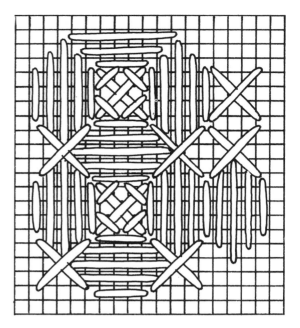

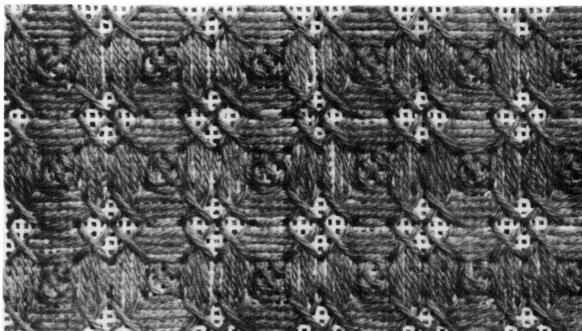

Rose — Overlapped

This is a more closely worked version of Rose Stitch, which completely covers the canvas, as shown in the diagram.

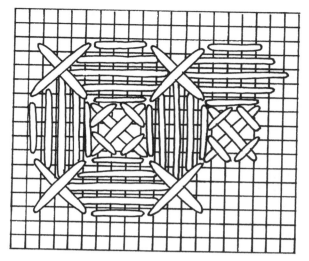

Roumanian Couching (Also known as Laid Oriental and Figure)

The needle is brought up at the top left-hand corner of the area to be covered, and the yarn is laid between two horizontal threads of the canvas across to the right-hand side. The needle is then brought up again at a point immediately beneath the laid yarn and two vertical threads of the canvas back to the left. The working yarn is taken over the top of the laid yarn and down again through the canvas at a point six vertical threads further to the left and immediately beneath the laid yarn. It is brought up again one vertical thread of the canvas further to the left, and the process of couching down is continued in the same way.

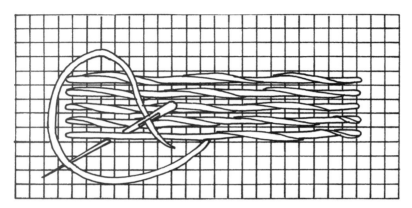

Satin

The name Satin Stitch covers a great variety of patterns which can be made by working a series of vertical, horizontal or diagonal straight stitches over any number of canvas threads. If a large area is to be worked in Satin Stitch, which is all in one colour, then it is good to remember that a pattern, in which there is a change in the direction of the stitch, will give more light and shade, than a pattern with all the stitches going in one direction. In this way even more variety can be given to a very versatile stitch. To obtain the best effect when working this stitch, the yarn must be evenly tensioned, and there must be as much yarn under the canvas as on top.

Satin Balloon

This stitch consists of groups of eight horizontal straight stitches over two, four, six, eight, eight, six, four and two vertical threads of the canvas respectively. The groups of stitches are fitted together to form an all-over pattern, with the longest stitches going into the same holes in the canvas as the shortest stitches in adjacent groups.

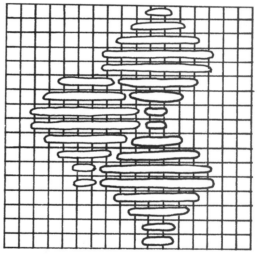

Satin Lozenge

Nine vertical straight stitches are first worked, proceeding from left to right over a series of one, two, three, four, five, six, seven, eight and nine horizontal threads of the canvas to form the shape of a right-angled triangle. Then a group of three vertical stitches, placed one above another, is worked to occupy the position beside the last long stitch over nine horizontal threads. This grouping of three vertical stitches is repeated twice more, before another group of nine vertical stitches, similar to the first such group, but proceeding from the longest to the shortest stitch, and forming the shape of a right-angled triangle in reverse, is now put in to complete the full lozenge shape. These shapes are worked in rows horizontally across the canvas, and subsequent rows are fitted in to produce the pattern shown in the diagram. This is quite a good stitch to use, when a large area has to be covered.

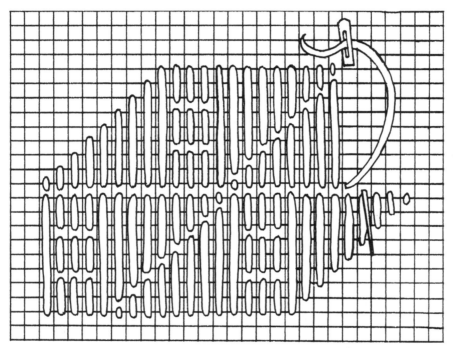

Satin Square. See Flat

Satin — Padded

A diamond shape is worked, which is composed of ten graduated horizontal straight stitches, divided down the centre. The individual stitches are worked over two, three, four, five, six, six, five, four, three and two threads of the canvas respectively. The yarn is then brought out of the canvas at the top left-hand side of the central division and is taken down under the right-hand block of stitches without going through the canvas. It is taken back up under the left-hand block of stitches, the process being repeated, until sufficient padding has been obtained. When the padding has been completed, the yarn is taken down through the canvas again at the same point from which it emerged.

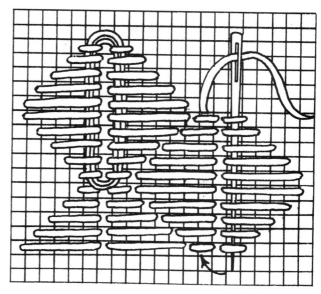

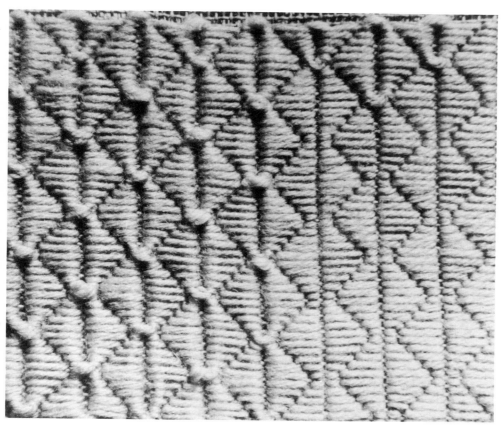

Satin Triangles

Triangular shapes are built up by working six horizontal straight stitches over a sequence of two, four, six, eight, ten and twelve vertical threads of the canvas. Rows of these shapes are worked horizontally across the area to be covered. Into the shapes which are left between these triangles others are fitted, consisting of eleven vertical straight stitches, worked over one, two, three, four, five, six, five, four, three, two and one horizontal threads of the canvas respectively. See the photograph.

Satin — Variation

This stitch-pattern starts with a cross stitch over two vertical and two horizontal threads of the canvas, which is then surrounded by eight back stitches over one thread of the canvas. Groups of five straight stitches, which are worked over two, three, four, three and two threads respectively, are then arranged to fit around the enclosed cross stitch and thus form a diamond shape, as shown in the diagram.

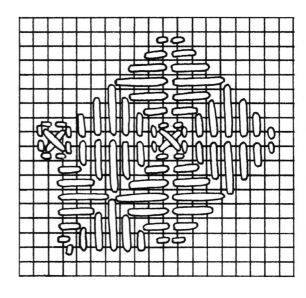

Scallop

This stitch is composed of seventeen individual
stitches, all of which go down into one hole in
the canvas at the centre of the base of the stitch.
A long vertical centre stitch is put in first over
twelve horizontal threads of the canvas. On
either side of this stitch are placed four other
stitches, which fan out, so that the top end of
each one of them is placed one intersection of
the canvas down to the right or to the left of the
previous stitch working from the centre outwards.
Finally four stitches are worked on either side,
which have their top ends placed one horizontal
thread below each other. Rows of these stitches
are worked horizontally across the area to be
covered, with succeeding rows fitting exactly into
the spaces in the rows before them.

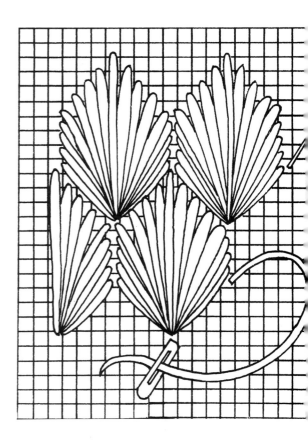

Scottish. See Cushion

Seven

This stitch consists of four vertical straight stitches, worked over four horizontal threads of the canvas, and crossed horizontally by three straight stitches over five vertical threads of the canvas. These groups of stitches are worked immediately below each other, and the two unworked threads left between groups can be filled, if necessary, with an upright cross stitch.

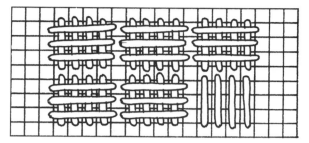

Sheaf

This stitch, which is always worked vertically upwards, needs a good, firm yarn to get the best results. It is worked in three stages. In the first stage a foundation of pairs of horizontal stitches is laid over the area to be covered, the spacing of these pairs of stitches depending upon the length of the 'sheaf' required. For the second stage the needle is brought up at the bottom right-hand corner of the stitch to be worked, just beneath the lower of two of the horizontal laid stitches and one thread in from the right-hand end, as shown in the diagram. A series of vertical Satin Stitches is then put in over two pairs of these laid stitches without entering the canvas, a sufficient number of stitches being worked to cover the laid bars adequately. The yarn is then brought up between stitches as at point A on the diagram and, still without entering the canvas, a second series of vertical Satin Stitches is worked — this time from left to right — over the second and third pair of laid bars, the lower end of each of this second series of stitches being taken between two stitches in the previous group. Care must be taken to see that each group of Satin Stitches interlocks correctly with the previous group. At the end of this second stage the needle, having taken the yarn up for the last Satin Stitch over the second and third pair of horizontal laid stitches, should go down through the canvas and be brought up again on the right of the spot where the Satin Stitchs interlock over the second pair of horizontal stitches — point B in the diagram — ready to commence the third stage.

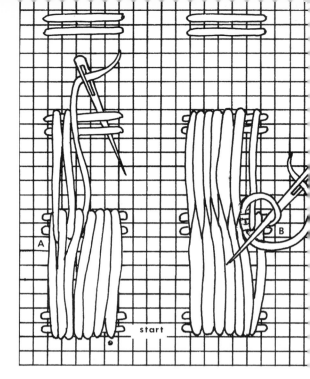

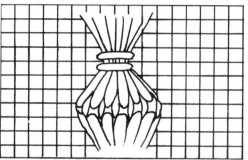

The third stage consists of taking the needle from the point where it emerged from the canvas up over the juncture of the first pair of Satin Stitches on that side and down behind it, as well as behind the horizontal laid stitches at that point, to come out and be slipped through the loop of the yarn, as shown in the diagram. The yarn is pulled tight to make a firm knot. This process is continued with each pair of Satin Stitches, until the opposite end of the horizontal bars is reached. This knotting, which is worked over each row of interlocked stitches, has the effect of fixing them firmly in place and also of fanning them out into shape. As the needle passes from one 'sheaf' to another, to work these knots, each 'sheaf' is tied in the centre with two horizontal stitches.

Shell

This stitch is worked like Wheatsheaf Stitch, see diagram, having three vertical straight stitches, tied down in the centre, but, as it always passes over an even number of horizontal threads of the canvas, it should be tied down by means of a back stitch and not a tent stitch. When a row of these stitches has been worked, adjacent ones are joined together by coiling the yarn through the back stitches one and a half times. See diagram.

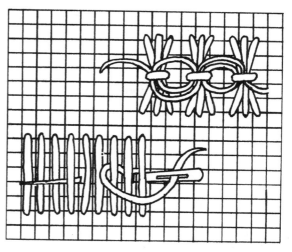

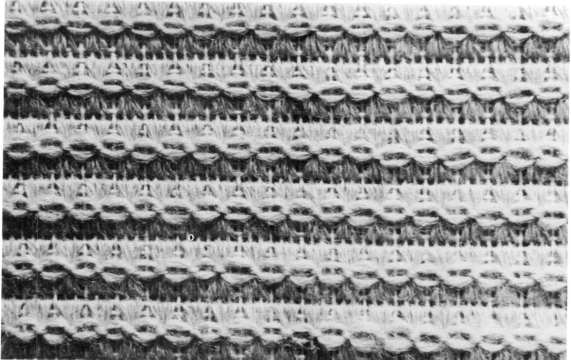

Single Scroll

This stitch is worked from left to right across the area to be covered. The yarn is brought up to the surface on the left-hand side and a loop is held down, whilst the needle is taken down through the canvas at a point two intersections up to the right of the hole from which the yarn first emerged, and it is brought up again two horizontal threads immediately below this point, and the yarn is drawn through the loop.

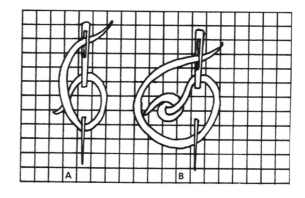

Six-sided Eye (Twenty-eight Stitch Hexagon)

This Eye Stitch has a hexagonal shape, formed by working five stitches from the top edge into a centre hole five horizontal threads of the canvas down. Five more stitches are taken down into the centrehole from intersections of the canvas running from the top edge of the stitch down to the left, and another similar group of stitches from the intersections running down to the right. The lower half of the hexagon is worked in a similar way from the reverse direction.

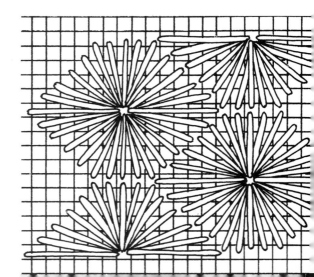

Small Grounding

This is, as its name implies, a useful stitch for working backgrounds. A cross stitch is worked first over four intersections of the canvas, and an oblique stitch is then taken from the centre hole, which is three horizontal threads of the canvas down from the top of the cross, up to a point one vertical thread to the right of the top left-hand corner of the cross. The yarn is brought out again, this time from the centre hole at the base of the cross, and it is taken up to a point, which is one horizontal thread of the canvas immediately below the top left-hand corner of the cross. This sequence of two oblique stitches is repeated on the other side of the cross, as is shown in the diagram. In the photograph this stitch is shown worked both over four threads of the canvas and also over eight threads, and it should be noted that an extra vertical stitch has

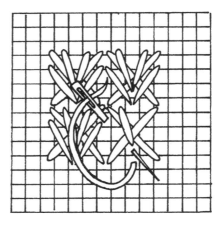

been worked in the larger version from the centre hole at the top of the cross down over three horizontal threads of the canvas.

Small Grounding

Smocking

Two groups of eight vertical stitches are worked
over two, four, six, six, eight, six, six and four
horizontal threads of the canvas, and two stitches
over six threads of the canvas, which are next to
one another, being both worked into the same
hole in the canvas in each case. The three centre
stitches in the group are then tied down in the
middle by two horizontal stitches, worked over
two vertical threads of the canvas, and the three
remaining stitches — those over six, four and
two threads — are tied down with the first three
stitches of the second group, which are over a
similar sequence of canvas threads, but in reverse,
by means of two horizontal stitches over four
threads of the canvas. In working the second row
of these stitches, the longest stitch in each group
is placed under the shortest stitch in the groups
in the previous row.

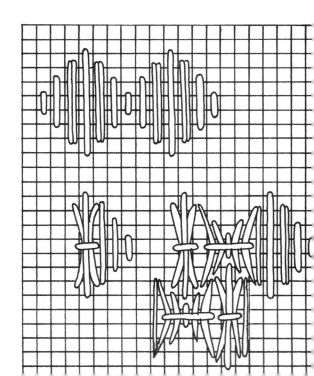

Smyrna (Also known as Double Cross or Leviathan)

This stitch consists of a diagonal cross stitch with an upright cross stitch worked over it. It can be worked over two, four or more even numbers of threads of the canvas and is a very useful stitch for working in conjunction with Rhodes Stitch, especially when a somewhat irregular shape has to be covered. The top stitches of the straight crosses should all be worked in one direction, either all horizontally or all vertically.

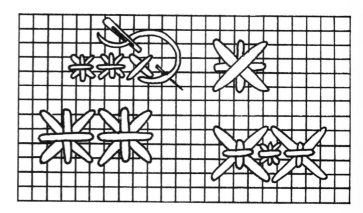

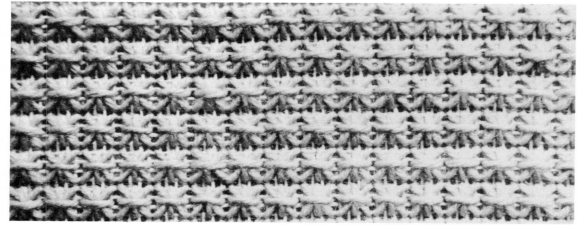

Smyrna Linked

In this variation of Smyrna Stitch two groups of stitches are worked together side by side. The vertical stitch of the upright cross is worked first, and then the diagonal cross is put in on top of it in each of the two groups of stitches. Finally, the two groups are joined together by means of one long horizontal stitch, which is taken right across the centre of them.

Snail's Trail. See Coral Zigzag

Spanish Knot (Also known as Feather)

This stitch is worked in vertical rows downwards over the area to be covered. The yarn is brought up two horizontal threads of the canvas below the top edge of the area to be worked and is held down with the left thumb, while the needle is taken down through the canvas at a point two horizontal threads above and one vertical thread to the left, and is brought out again four horizontal threads down and two vertical threads to the left, to be taken through the loop of the yarn, as shown at A in the diagram. The needle is again taken down through the canvas at a point one horizontal thread immediately above where the first stitch was started, and is brought out four horizontal threads down and two vertical threads to the right, where it is pulled through the loop of the yarn, as shown at B in the diagram. A loop of the yarn is then taken over to the left and is held down by the left thumb as before, while the needle is taken down through the canvas at a point three horizontal threads immediately below where the first stitch started and is brought out again three horizontal threads down and three vertical threads to the left, where it is taken through the loop of the yarn, as in working the first stitch (See C in the diagram). The fourth stage in the working process is shown at D in the diagram, where the yarn is again looped to the right and held in position, while the needle is taken down through the canvas at a point four horizontal threads immediately below the beginning of the first stitch, and is brought out three horizontal threads down and two vertical threads to the right, to be taken through the loop of the yarn.

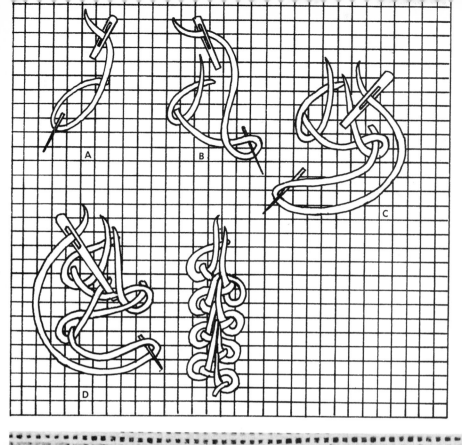

Spring

This useful little stitch starts with the working of a vertical group of seven horizontal stitches, each stitch being worked over three vertical threads of the canvas. The first stitch in this group is put in three horizontal threads down from the top of the area to be covered, and, when the complete group of seven stitches has been worked, the yarn is brought up through the canvas at a point three horizontal threads immediately below the left-hand end of the last of these seven stitches and it is taken up under the group of stitches to work a long oblong cross stitch over three vertical and twelve horizontal threads, which extends to a

point three horizontal threads above the first horizontal stitch in the group, as shown in the diagram. Another similar group of stitches is put in immediately below the first, and the process is repeated until the bottom of the first vertical row is reached. A small cross stitch, worked over one vertical and two horizontal threads of the canvas is then placed between the 'V' shapes formed at each end of the groups of stitches already worked. The second row of stitches is worked in the same way, but the groups of seven horizontal stitches are placed three horizontal threads of the canvas below their position in the first row.

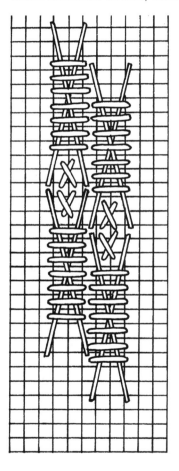

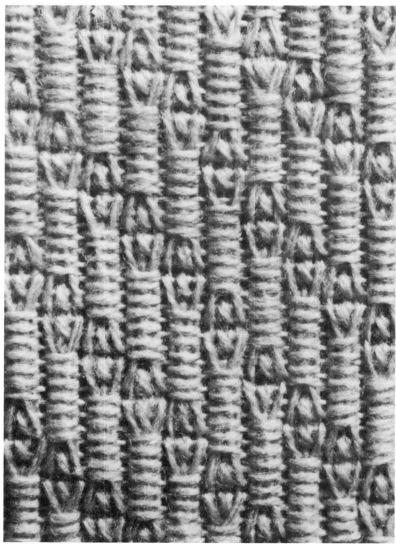

Star

Upright cross stitches, worked over six horizontal and six vertical threads of the canvas, form the basis of this stitch, with a diagonal cross stitch over four horizontal and four vertical threads worked over the centre of each upright cross. After a grid of these stitches has been worked over the area to be covered, upright cross stitches over six horizontal and six vertical threads of the canvas are placed between them, and each of these upright crosses is itself crossed in the centre by a small diagonal cross stitch, worked over two horizontal and two vertical threads of the canvas.

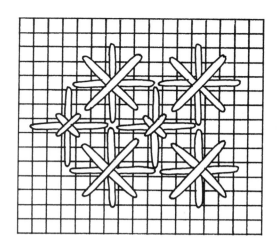

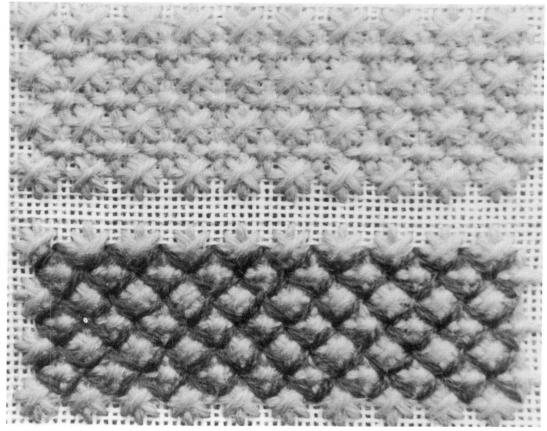

Stem or Outline

This is generally regarded as a crewel work stitch to be used solely on a silk, cotton or linen ground and is seldom seen worked as a modern canvas work stitch. It is useful, however, as an outlining stitch and will also cover the canvas well, when used as a filling stitch.

The method of working is the same as is used for crewel work: a long stitch is taken over a number of canvas threads, and the yarn is brought out again beside this stitch and half-way back along its length, before moving forward once more.

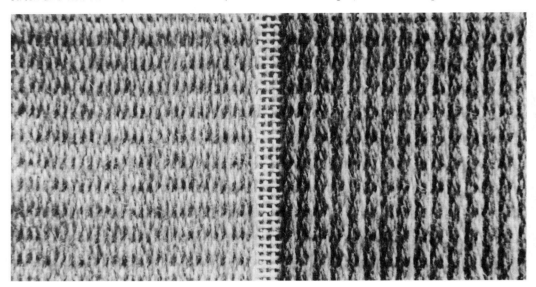

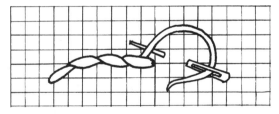

Stem — Broad

This stitch is very similar to Knitting Stitch. It is an oblique stitch, worked over two or more intersections of the canvas in vertical rows, using every other hole in the canvas and alternating the direction of the stitches in adjacent rows. A back stitch is taken over two horizontal threads between the rows.

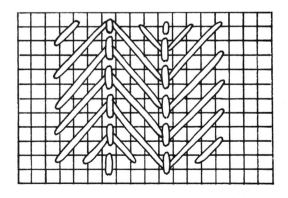

Stocking. See Knitted 2

Straight Cross. See Cross, Straight

Sunburst

From the centre hole at the base of this stitch four individual stitches radiate to the left and four to the right. One horizontal stitch over six vertical threads of the canvas follows the base-line to the left and a similar stitch is taken to the right. The other three stitches, which radiate from the centre hole to either side, finish directly above the ends of the base-line stitches and have a space of two horizontal threads between them.

A vertical row of these stitches is worked from top to bottom of the area to be covered. Then a wrapping-round yarn, which could be slightly thicker than the yarn used for the first part of the stitch, is brought up through the canvas at a point on the base-line of the first stitch, which is two vertical threads of the canvas to the left of the centre hole. It is wrapped once round under this stitch in an anti-clockwise direction, and is then taken down under the left-hand side of the second stitch, to be wrapped once round under that stitch in the same way. This process is continued down to the bottom of the row of stitches, with the yarn being wrapped once round each stitch in the row. When the end of the row has been reached, the yarn is taken up under the right-hand side of all the stitches to the top of the row, where it is passed behind the top stitch and is taken down through the canvas into the same hole on the left, from which it emerged.

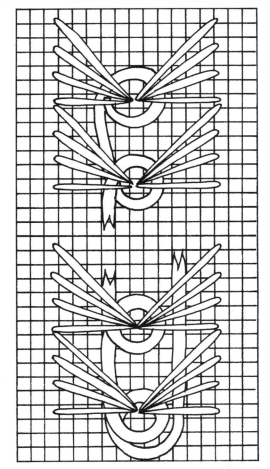

The second row of these stitches is so placed that it overlaps the previous row by one vertical thread of the canvas.

Surrey

This is a pile stitch similar to the Ghiordes Knot,
but the method of working is different. As is the
case with all cut stitches, this stitch is worked
from the bottom row upwards. The end of the
working yarn is left on the surface, when the
needle is taken down through the canvas. It is
brought up again two horizontal threads of the
canvas immediately below, and a stitch is put in
over two intersections of the canvas up to the
right. The needle is then brought out two vertical
threads to the left, from the same hole by which
the yarn first entered the canvas and through the
loop of the yarn. The latter is then tightened.
To work the second stitch the needle is taken
down through the canvas two vertical threads to
the right, into the same hole as the top end of the
last diagonal stitch, leaving a loop of yarn on the
surface. The process is then continued in the same
way as described above. The loops which are
formed can either be cut short or left uncut.

Work from the bottom upwards

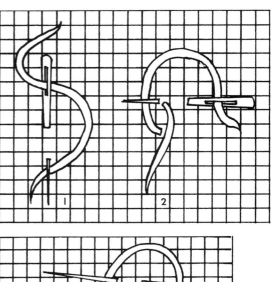

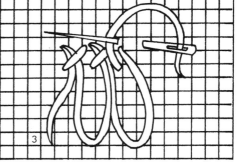

Swedish Cross

The shape of a cross is formed by the working of long-legged cross stitch in varying lengths across the canvas from left to right, as shown in the diagram. The actual size of the cross shape, which is developed in this way, can be varied as desired. It makes a quite decorative piece of stitchery, which may be used with success in conjunction with a smaller stitch, such as Mosaic or Tent Stitch.

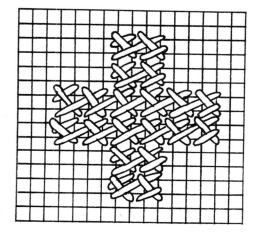

Tent (Also known as Petit Point and Continental Stitch)

Tent Stitch and Back Stitch are the two smallest stitches which it is possible to use on canvas. The only difference between these two stitches is that Tent Stitch is always worked over one intersection of the canvas and Back Stitch is a straight stitch, which is worked between the threads of the canvas, generally over two horizontal or two vertical threads. The correct way of working Tent Stitch is shown in detail in the diagram. This shows the correct positioning of the needle, when working the stitch in different directions.

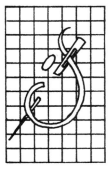

Tent Stitch worked from the top downwards

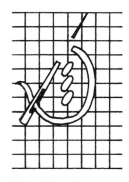

Worked from bottom upwards

Tent Stitch worked horizontally across the canvas

Tent Stitch worked diagonally across the canvas

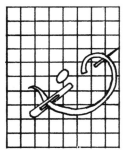

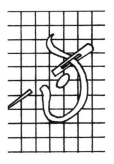

Working from left to right

Working from right to left

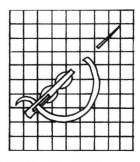

Working Tent Stitch diagonally up from bottom left-hand to top right-hand

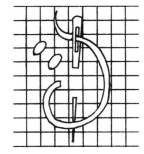

Working Tent Stitch diagonally from top left downwards to bottom right-hand

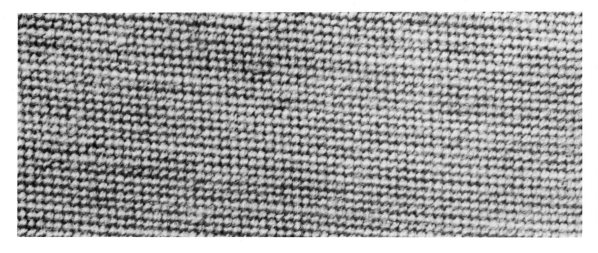

Tent — Reversed

This variation of Tent Stitch is worked in the same way as normal Tent Stitch, but the stitches in alternate rows are sloped in the reverse direction from the normal as shown in the diagram. The finished effect of this stitch is much improved, if alternate rows are worked in a different colour from that used for the other rows.

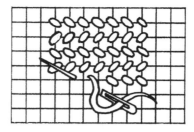

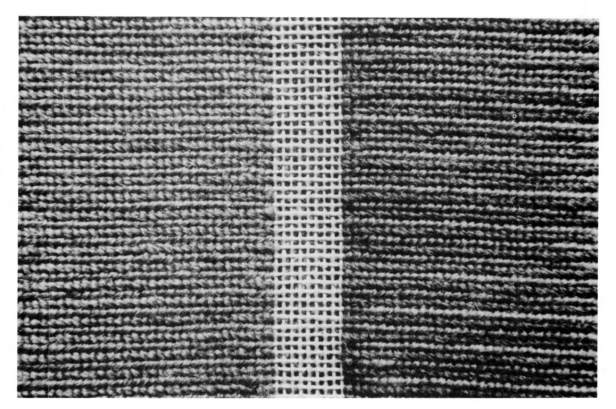

Tent, Woven. See Woven Tent

Tied Coral. See Palestrina

Tile

This square stitch is based on a diagonal cross stitch over two threads of the canvas, which is surrounded on all four sides by back stitches, worked over two threads. Lines of tent stitch are worked both horizontally and vertically to enclose the rows of cross stitches, whilst leaving a single thread of unworked canvas around each one.

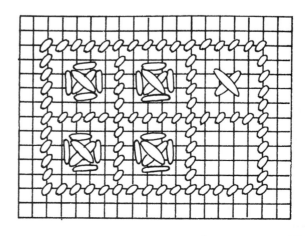

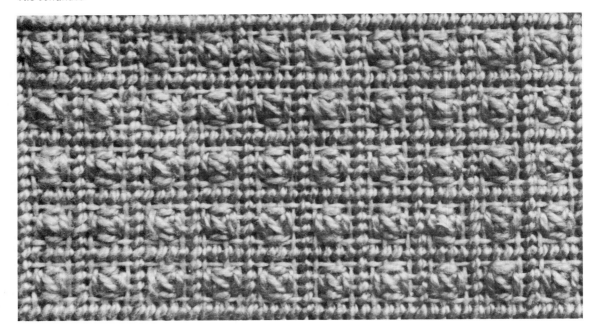

Triangular Two-sided. See Turkish Two-Sided

Triple Cross

A diagonal cross stitch over four vertical and four horizontal threads of the canvas is worked first. The needle is then brought out at the bottom right-hand corner of the cross and is taken down at a point four horizontal threads up and two vertical threads to the left, into the centre hole between the two top arms of the cross. It is brought out again at the bottom left-hand corner of the cross and is taken down into the same centre hole at the top with the previous stitch. Then the needle is brought out at a point four horizontal threads below, from the centre hole between the two lower arms of the cross, and is taken down at the top right-hand corner of the cross. Finally the needle is again brought out at the centre hole at the base of the stitch and is taken down at the top left-hand corner of the cross.

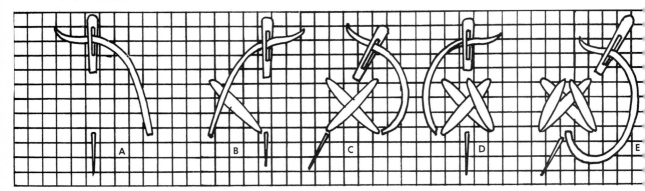

Triple Cross Encroaching

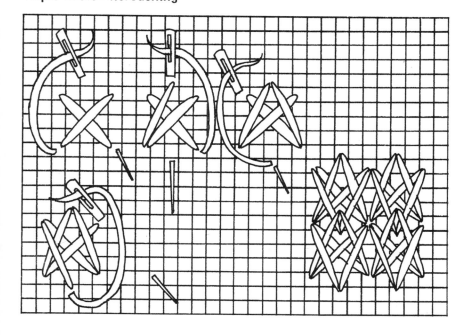

Triple Cross Encroaching continued

This stitch is the same as Triple Cross Stitch, except that, as the name implies, it encroaches over the stitch above it in the previous row and so makes a good filling stitch. The working starts, as before, with a cross stitch over four threads of the canvas, but the individual stitches forming the 'Vee' shapes, which are worked over the cross, are over five horizontal and two vertical threads, instead of four and two threads. This means that, when a second or subsequent row of stitches is being worked, the 'Vee' shape encroaches over the stitch above it by one thread of the canvas. See the diagram.

Triple Twist

This stitch begins with the working of a cross stitch over eight horizontal and four vertical threads of the canvas. A second cross stitch over eight horizontal and two vertical threads is worked on top of the first cross, so that the ends of its individual stitches are placed one vertical thread inside those of the first cross. A third cross stitch over six horizontal and four vertical threads is then worked on top of the other two crosses, with the ends of its individual stitches placed one horizontal thread above or below those of the first cross thus completing a perfectly symmetrical triple cross.

Rows of this stitch can be worked horizontally or vertically across the canvas, but it probably looks best when it is worked diagonally downwards with a half-drop.

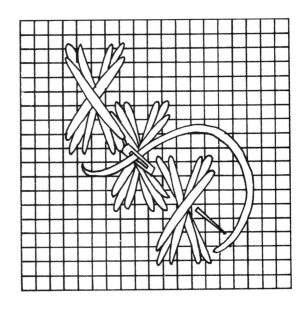

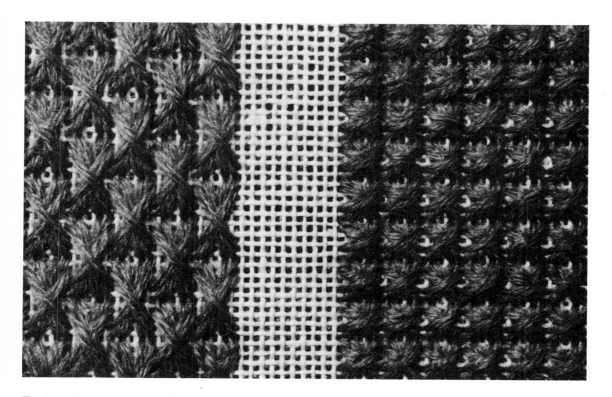

Turkey Rug Knot. See Ghiordes Knot

Turkish Two-sided (Also known as Triangular Two-sided)

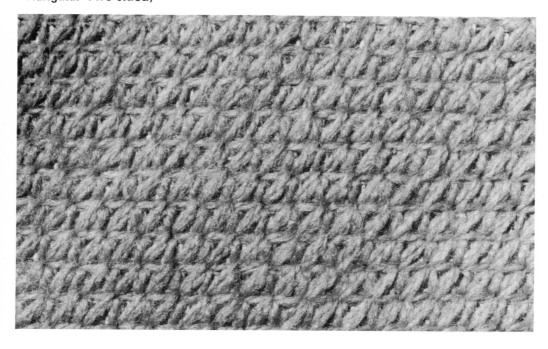

Turkish Two-sided continued

This stitch is worked diagonally from the bottom left-hand corner up to the right, and then back again. The diagram shows the different stages in the working. It also shows the stitch worked over four threads of the canvas, but this number may be varied, as is seen in the photograph of the worked sampler. A series of vertical straight stitches over four horizontal threads is shown at A in the diagram, the individual stitches being separated from one another by four vertical threads of the canvas, and each one starting four horizontal threads higher than the previous one. The needle is brought up four vertical threads to the right of the top end of the last vertical stitch in the row, and a horizontal stitch over four

vertical threads is put in, going back to the same hole at the top of the last vertical stitch (see B in the diagram). Then the needle is brought out at the bottom of this stitch, four horizontal threads down, and is taken back up to the right over four intersections of the canvas, to form a triangular shape (see C in the diagram). It is once more brought out at the top of the next vertical stitch back to the left, and a diagonal stitch is taken up to the right over four intersections of the canvas (see D in the diagram). The needle goes down into the hole at the top of the last vertical stitch in the row and comes up again at the lower end of this stitch, ready to continue the process.

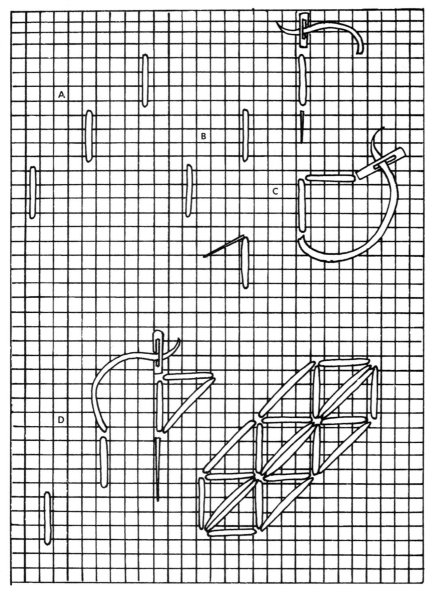

Turkish Two-sided — Horizontal

The diagram clearly shows the working of this
horizontal variation of Turkish Two-sided Stitch.
It is a useful stitch to work with two different
coloured yarns.

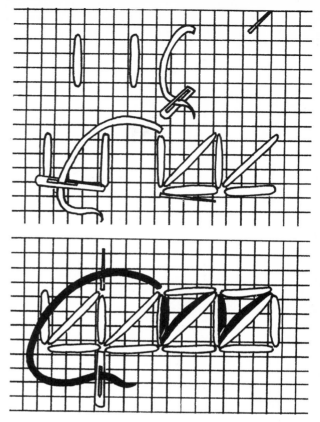

Two-colour variation

Turkish — Variation

This stitch is similar to Turkish Two-sided Stitch,
but it is worked horizontally and not diagonally
across the canvas, and it has four extra stitches.
These are four back stitches, which are worked
over two threads of the canvas, and form a small
square shape inside the larger square of the two-
sided stitch, before the diagonal stitches are put
in over them as shown in the diagram.

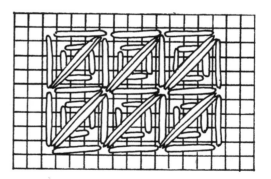

Tweed

This stitch consists of an upright cross stitch over
six threads of the canvas, which has been crossed
in the centre by a diagonal cross, worked over two
threads. It is worked in rows horizontally across
the area to be covered, with subsequent rows being
fitted in between the stitches in the previous
row. A tiny diagonal cross stitch over one vertical
and one horizontal thread is worked in each of
the empty spaces left between the large crosses.
If two shades of yarn are used in the working, an
attractive tweedy effect can be achieved.

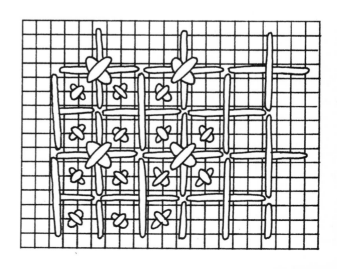

Tweed continued

Twill

Vertical straight stitches, over three or more horizontal threads of the canvas, are worked in rows diagonally downwards across the canvas, with each individual stitch dropping down one or two threads lower than the stitch before it. This gives the appearance of a woven twill. The thickness of the yarn must be matched to the type of canvas used, in order that the surface may be completely covered.

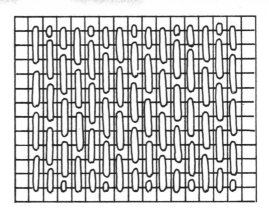

Twill — Double

This stitch is formed by working diagonal rows of vertical straight stitches over four horizontal threads of the canvas, alternating with rows of similar stitches over two horizontal threads. This makes a very good filling stitch, provided that the yarn used is of the correct thickness to cover the canvas well.

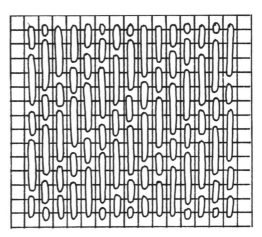

Twisted Chain. See Chain, Twisted

Two-sided

A long oblique stitch over nine horizontal and three vertical threads of the canvas is taken up to the right. The yarn is brought out three intersections of the canvas down to the left, and a horizontal stitch over six vertical threads is then put in to the right. The needle is brought up three intersections of the canvas up to the left, from the hole at the top of the first long oblique stitch, and another similar stitch is taken down to the right over nine horizontal and three vertical threads. The yarn is then brought out three intersections of the canvas up to left, and a diagonal stitch is worked up to the left over three intersections of the canvas, the needle going down into the hole at the left-hand end of the horizontal stitch. It is brought out again from the hole at the point where the last stitch started, and another diagonal stitch over three intersections of the canvas is taken up to the right, into the hole at the right-hand end of the horizontal stitch. The yarn is brought up three intersections of the canvas down to the left, from the same hole from which the diagonal stitches started, and another horizontal stitch over six vertical threads is put in going to the right, the needle being brought out three intersections of the canvas down to the left, from the hole at the lower end of the second long oblique stitch, ready to start the sequence of stitches over again.

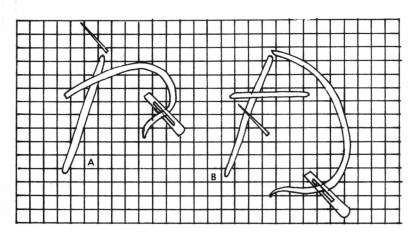

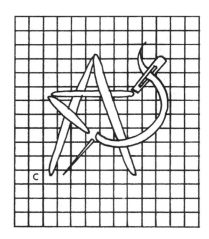

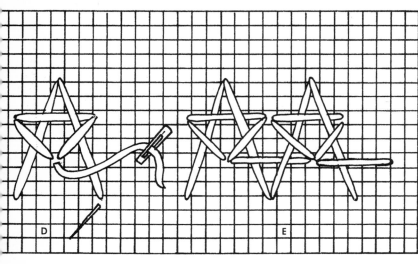

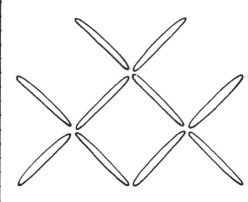

Back view of stitch

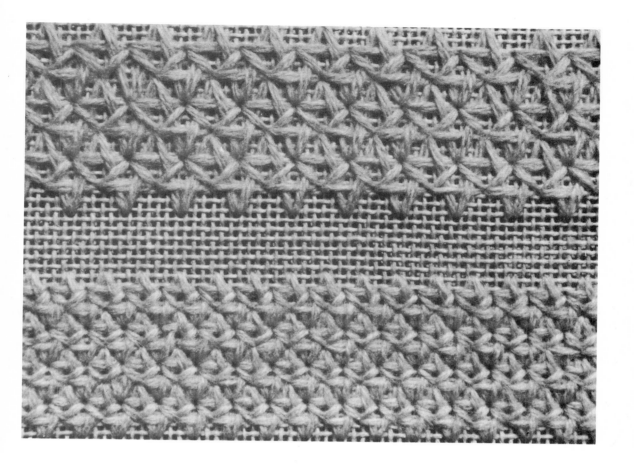

Upright Cross. See Cross, Upright

Vandyke

This stitch can be worked over any number of threads of the canvas, as is shown in the photograph, but the diagram shows it worked over an area of five vertical and three horizontal threads. It is worked in vertical rows from the top downwards. The needle is brought up three horizontal threads of the canvas down on the left-hand side of the area to be covered, and a diagonal stitch is taken up to the right over three intersections of the canvas. The needle is brought up again one

vertical thread to the left, and another diagonal stitch is taken down to the right over three intersections of the canvas. The next stitch begins two horizontal threads below the first stitch, but this time, instead of taking the yarn down through the canvas, the needle is slipped under the crossed yarn of the first stitch in the centre, as is shown in the diagram. Other stitches are then worked in this way to complete the row. This is a useful stitch for working shapes such as leaves, as the size of the individual stitches can be varied.

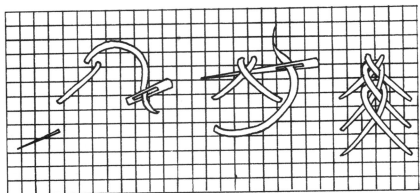

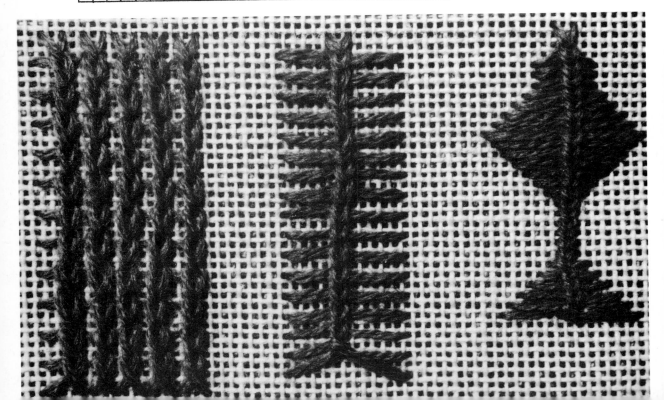

Vee

This stitch consists of groups of nine individual stitches, all going down into a central hole in the canvas at the base of the group, with the groups being worked in vertical columns, proceeding from the top of the canvas downwards. The basic group of individual stitches begins with a vertical straight stitch over four horizontal threads of the canvas. On either side of this central stitch four oblique stitches are also taken down into the same hole at its base from points around a semi-circular shape, the first and lowest stitch on either side from a point one horizontal thread above and five vertical threads to the right or left of the centre hole, the second stitch from a point three horizontal threads above and five vertical threads to right or left, the third stitch from a point five horizontal threads above and four vertical threads to right or left and the fourth and final stitch in the group from a point eight horizontal threads above the base and four vertical threads to right or left of the centre hole.

In placing subsequent Vee Stitches beneath the others in a vertical row, the working begins with the central vertical stitch being taken from a point four horizontal threads of the canvas immed-iately below the centre hole in the base of the group above and consequently going down into this same hole. This means that the longest individual stitches on either side of the subsequent groups of stitches overlap the two lowest stitches on either side of previous groups.

The photograph shows how in the worked example of Vee Stitch the two longest individual oblique stitches in each of the top groups is reduced from eight horizontal threads above the base to five, in order to fit into the canvas. These shortened stitches (sometimes called compensation stitches) are shown with broken lines in the diagram.

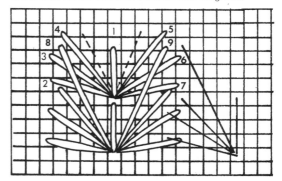

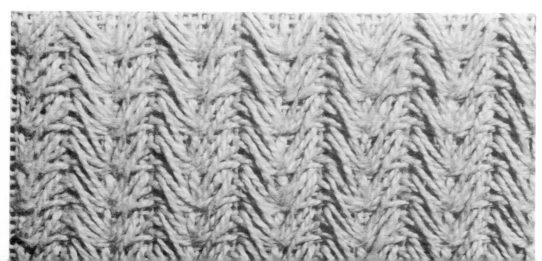

Velvet

This stitch is worked in horizontal rows from left to right, beginning at the bottom edge of the area to be covered and working upwards. A diagonal stitch over two intersections of the canvas is taken up to the right, and the needle is then brought out again at the starting hole. A loop of yarn is formed and held in place, whilst the needle is once more taken down into the same hole at the top of the first stitch and brought up again two horizontal threads of the canvas directly below. A diagonal stitch is then taken up over the loop of the yarn and over two intersections of the canvas to the left, and the needle is brought out at the same hole from which this last stitch had started, ready to start the second stitch.

The loops of yarn may be worked over a gauge, such as a knitting pin, or something similar, in order to ensure that they are all the same length. They are cut, when the working is finished, and the pile is trimmed as required. A row of cross stitches, worked, as shown in the diagram, down the sides of the area that has been covered, helps to keep the cut pile looking trim at the edges.

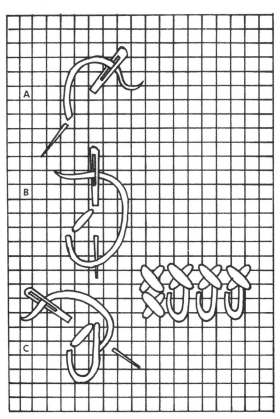

Work from bottom row up to top

Victorian Tufting

The basis of this stitch is Herringbone Stitch, which is worked over every thread of the canvas in order to give complete security to the work. One row of Herringbone Stitch, worked over one thread of the canvas, is first put in along one side of the central square, as shown in the diagram. The second row is worked over the top of the first row, with the individual stitches being put in over three threads of the canvas, and starting one horizontal thread below the stitches in the first row and extending to a point one horizontal thread above them. Succeeding rows of stitches are made in the same way, ie each individual stitch begins one horizontal thread below the corresponding stitch in the previous row and extends to a point one horizontal thread above

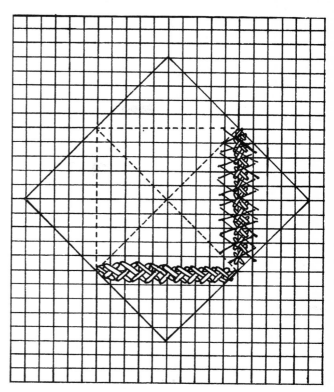

This size gives a small diamond shape of approximately 2.5 cm (1 in.) when worked over 21 canvas threads

this stitch. The rows of stitches are worked so as to fit into the diamond shape shown in the diagram. Four of these small diamond shapes are worked in this way to give the shape of a square with four triangles surrounding it. None of the four diamond shapes should be cut until all four have been completely worked, or chaos will ensue. If a row of Tent Stitch is worked all round the shape first, this will help, not only to hold the pile better, but also to make the finished piece of work have a neater appearance. The final part of the process is to cut each stitch in the middle and then to trim the pile to the required length. The reverse side of the work shows close rows of Back Stitch.

Victorian Tufting — Circular

To work a small circle

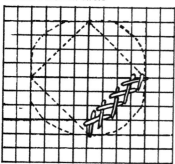

Waffle. See Norwich

Web

This stitch is somewhat similar to Bokhara couching, but it is worked diagonally across the canvas, and generally on a double-mesh canvas. To start working this stitch, a length of yarn is laid diagonally across the area to be covered. If a double-mesh canvas is being used, the yarn is laid diagonally over the large holes, and a small stitch over the intersections is used to tie it down. When it is completely tied down, the next length of yarn is laid. The diagram shows the working of the stitch on both double-mesh and single-mesh canvas.

On single mesh canvas

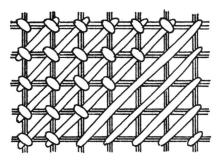

On double mesh canvas

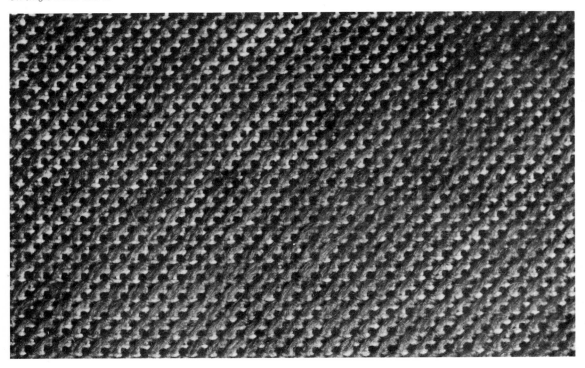

Wheatsheaf

This stitch consists of three vertical straight stitches, taken over four or more horizontal threads of the canvas. When these three stitches are over an even number of canvas threads, the needle is next brought up in the centre hole to the left, and the yarn is taken over the three stitches to the right and down again into the same hole. If, however, the three stitches pass over an uneven number of canvas threads, they can be tied down with a tent stitch. When Wheatsheaf Stitch is used for an all-over filling stitch, it is advisable to work it in rows diagonally downwards as a half-drop pattern.

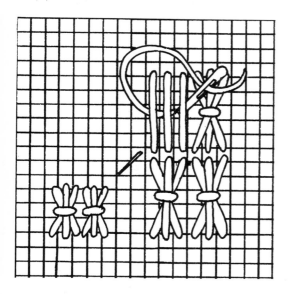

Wheatsheaf — Expanding

This variation of Wheatsheaf Stitch is very useful for working in a decorative manner and for filling irregular shapes in a design. It can also be used when a wavy line is needed, as is shown in the photograph.

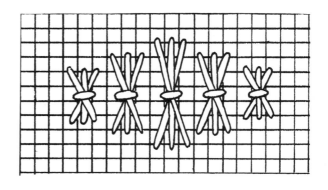

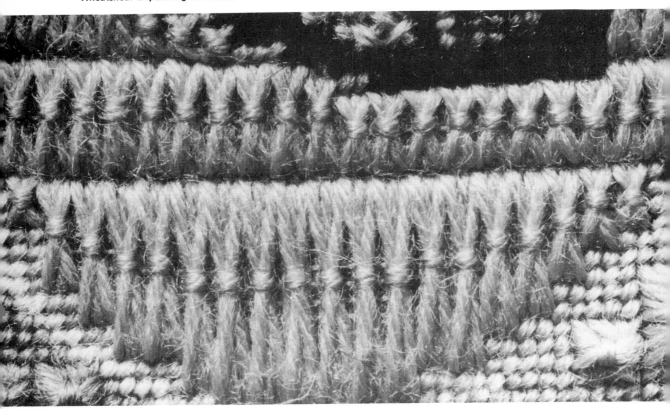

Wheatsheaf — Undulating

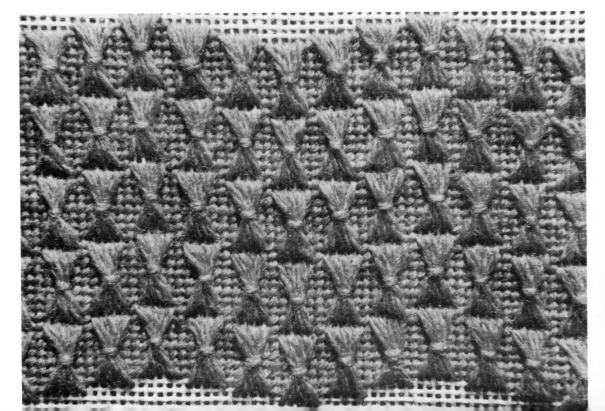

Woven Eye

The basis of this stitch is an Algerian Eye Stitch.
The diagram shows it worked over a square of six
threads of the canvas, but it can be worked to any
size that is required. The yarn is brought out one
thread below the centre hole of the Algerian Eye
Stitch, just beside the lower vertical stitch of the
eye, and is woven over this stitch to the left,
under the next stitch, and so on right round the
eye stitch, until it comes back to the point from
which it started. Then the yarn is taken back over
the lower diagonal stitch on the right of the eye
stitch, and under it and the next bar to the left.
This process of weaving back over one bar of the
eye and forward under two bars is continued
right round the eye stitch for as many times as is
necessary to cover all the bars of the eye completely. The greater number of times the yarn is
woven around the eye, the more raised will be the
final form of the stitch. These woven eyes can be
worked in rows, or they can be placed as shown
in the diagram, so that they will cover the canvas
somewhat better.

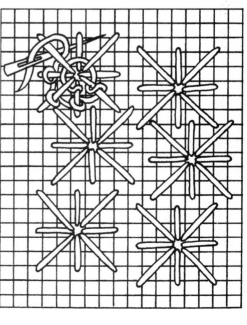

Woven Tent

This is an attractive new small stitch, which is based on a square of sixteen tent stitches. Two long stitches are put in, one, over four horizontal threads of the canvas, down the right-hand side of each square, and one, over four vertical threads, along the base of each square. These two stitches form the basis for the yarn to be interwoven backwards and forwards diagonally across one corner of each tent stitch square, as shown in the diagram.

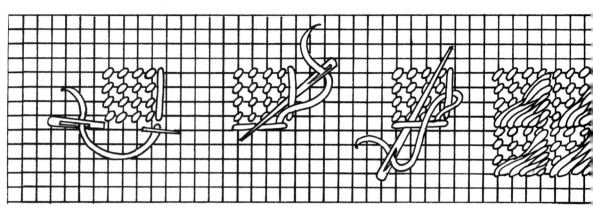

Woven Trellis

This stitch is based on a square of eight threads of the canvas. From each corner of this square three stitches are taken down into the centre hole, one a diagonal stitch over four intersections of the canvas, with the other two stitches starting from points one thread on either side of it. The yarn is then brought up through the centre hole in the canvas and is woven over and under the individual stitches of each of the four groups in turn, so that it completely covers them from the centre to the edge of the square.

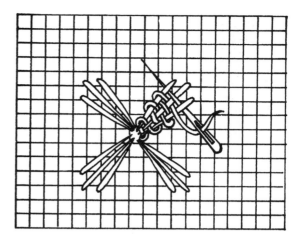

Zigzag

This stitch is worked from the bottom left-hand corner of the area to be covered and goes up to the right in diagonal rows of stepped back stitches. A vertical back stitch over two horizontal threads of the canvas is worked first, followed by a horizontal back stitch over two vertical threads. The second row of stitches starts two vertical threads of the canvas to the right, and the first vertical stitch goes down into the hole in the canvas at the right-hand end of the first horizontal stitch in the previous row. To obtain the maximum zigzag effect, it is essential to use different shades of colour in alternate diagonal rows of the stitch.

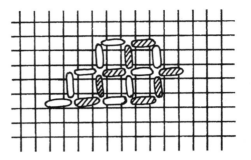

Zigzag Knotted. See Knotted Zigzag